THE VERSATILITY
OF CHAIRS

THE VERSATILITY OF CHAIRS

A THEATRICAL MEMOIR

EDWARD PIZZELLA

Library of Congress Control Number: 2014905936
ISBN: Hardcover   978-1-4931-9158-1
               Softcover   978-1-4931-9159-8
               eBook   978-1-4931-9157-4

This book was printed in the United States of America.

Rev. date: 04/26/2014

To order additional copies of this book, contact:
Xlibris LLC
1-888-795-4274
www.Xlibris.com
Orders@Xlibris.com
609966

CONTENTS

APPENDIX

DEDICATION

This work is dedicated to my two theatrical mentors, my first wife, Marge Pizzella, who encouraged me to become an actor, and Ray Shinn, an actor, director and founder of the Hole In The Wall Theatre of New Britain, who coached me on many of the basics of live theatre, both of whom, unfortunately, are now deceased.

To them I owe all that I have accomplished on stage. Marge was both a wonderful mother and an accomplished actress. It was she who first dared me to accept a bit role in a comedy, when an actor suddenly walked out of a show a few days prior to opening night. I thereafter experienced the pleasure of sharing leading roles with her in three comedies produced by Theatre Newington, the local community theatre group. We played opposite each other in "Time Out For Ginger," "Critic's Choice" and "You Know I Can't Hear You When The Water's Running."

And it was Ray Shinn who introduced me to the Hole In The Wall Theatre, as Lord Caversham in "An Ideal Husband" and thereafter instructed me in the timing and delivery of the brilliant comedic one-liners of the inimitable Neil Simon. I grew to understand and admire Ray and I cherished his criticism.

AUTHOR'S BIO

 Ed Pizzella is a lawyer, politician, consumer advocate, actor, director, producer, writer and, last but not least, a poet. A child of the Great Depression, Mr. Pizzella is the offspring of Italian immigrants. Born in the Italian ghetto of Hartford, Connecticut, he attended local public schools, where, by his heritage, he was driven to learn. Because he was born only a year after his mother arrived in this country, in his early years he spoke only Italian. He soon mastered English and at Northeast Junior High School in Hartford was elected to the National Honor Society, won the school's oratorical contest and was a graduation speaker and a recipient of the Civitan Award.

His appreciation of poetry commenced in his eighth grade English class, where he studied the classics and excelled in recitation. He was attracted to languages and avidly studied Latin, French and Italian. He also acquired a profound interest in mythology.

At Weaver High School in Hartford he wrote for the school newspaper, served as president of the French Club, was awarded the chemistry prize at graduation and ranked in the upper ten percent of his class. At Trinity College (Hartford) he majored in Romance Languages and in 1954 was graduated cum laude with a Bachelor of Arts degree. He received his Juris Doctor degree from the University of Connecticut School of Law in 1957, where he was graduated third in his class. He was admitted to the Connecticut Bar in 1957 and since that time has been actively engaged in the general practice of law.

While in law school, as a member of the Board of Student Editors (Law Review), he authored three articles which were published in the Connecticut Bar Journal. The last of the three, entitled "A Survey Of Connecticut Zoning Law," was subsequently republished in pamphlet form.

He was admitted to the Connecticut Bar in 1957 and is a member of the Connecticut Bar Association, the Federal District Court Bar for the District of Connecticut, the Second Circuit Court of Appeals Bar and the U. S. Supreme Court Bar.

He commenced legal practice as assistant legal aid attorney for the Legal Aid Society of Hartford County and, after he left that position to enter private practice, founded and chaired the Legal Aid Board of New Britain. He continued to hone his writing skills in the form of brief writing in the course of his extensive appellate practice. Writing became prominent in his civic and political activities, where, as President of the local Chamber of Commerce and as a local elected official, he penned numerous articles which were published in local newspapers.

He served as a member of the Newington Zoning Commission and as Chairman of the Zoning Board of Appeals. Upon his re-election, as a member of the Newington Town Council, received the highest number of votes. He also served as counsel for the Senate majority in the 1973 and 1974 state legislative sessions and in 1974, as counsel for the legislature's Banks and Regulated Activities Committee. In 1975 he was nominated as Newington's Republican candidate for Mayor and in 1995 as the Republican candidate for Probate Judge for the Newington Probate District.

In the late 1960's, Mr. Pizzella became active in community theatre and subsequently appeared in major roles in more than a hundred dinner theatre and community theatre productions in central Connecticut. He directed a number of theatrical productions for Theatre Newington and the Downstairs Cabaret in Newington, Connecticut, The OnStage

Performers in Wolcott, Connecticut, L'Auberge d'Elegance Dinner Theatre in Bristol, Connecticut, Beckley Dinner Theatre and The Connecticut Cabaret in Berlin, Connecticut, The Ramada Dinner Theatre in New Britain, Connecticut, and The Centre Stage Dinner Theatre in Meriden, Connecticut.

As one of the founders of Theatre One Productions, Inc., he assisted in producing nineteen major shows. He served as Business Manager for Theatre Newington, Secretary of Theatre One Productions, Chairman of the Tri-Town Community Cable Access Committee, Chairman of the Cox Cable Advisory Council and Vice-Chairman of the SNET State-wide Cable Advisory Council. He was a founder and served as Secretary of Newington Community Television, Inc., a local community access telecaster. He authored three theatrical reviews which were published in area newspapers. Many of his poems have been published in newspapers, on the internet and in anthologies.

A detailed theatrical resume can be found in the Appendix.

CHAPTER ONE

FROM DARE TO ADDICTION

"My God! You'll never guess what just happened!" She was frantic. "A week 'til opening night and he walks out! Can you believe it? He just walks out!" I could see that my normally self-controlled wife had lost it. She was utterly exasperated. I entreated her to simmer down and explain what had happened. "Our current show, 'Suds In Your Eye,'— you know, the one that opens a week from now," she said sarcastically, "well, everything was going great. We were coming into the home stretch and everything was shaping up. All of a sudden, one of the actors walks out! He's the guy who was playing the role of John Fitzgerald, you know, the Irish tax collector. We open in seven days! What the hell am I going to do?"

She was the president of Theatre Newington, the local community theatre group and, in precarious situations such as this, she occupied the unenviable position in which the proverbial buck, having whimsically circumnavigated in its inimitable fashion, would, with an intolerable screech, inevitably stop.

My next remark, I now admit, was either naïve or stupid, or perhaps a mixture of both. "Don't you have an understudy?" She exploded. "Where the hell have you been? Where have you ever seen an understudy in community theatre?" She was so agitated that I cautiously retreated to a neutral corner.

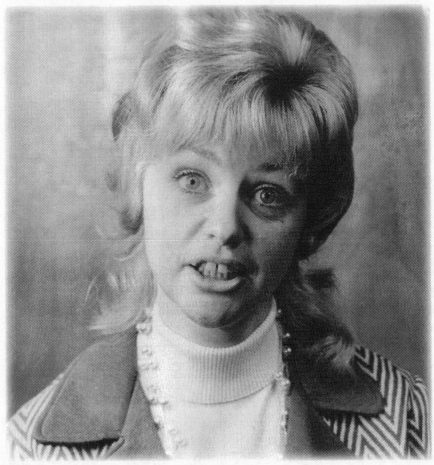

Marge Pizzella

She took a deep breath and her tension began to ease. "I've called everybody I can think of," she said, almost in tears. "It's a bit part, but I still can't get any takers! I'm at my wits' end!" "It shouldn't be that difficult," I offered, hoping that reasoning with her might calm her down. "Not that difficult? Are you crazy?" Now she was back to screaming. "If it's such a breeze, why don't you do it? I dare you," she taunted. "Me?" I laughed. "I've never even set foot on stage; not in a play, that is." There was a momentary, silent pause. We stared at each other for what seemed an eternity. "Me on stage? In a play? That's ridiculous," I thought.

Outwardly, I laughed hysterically, but inside my feverish skull my brain was racing. It was a sunny spring afternoon. I had just come home with a note from my teacher. I was in the fourth grade at the Brackett School on Westland Street in Hartford's north end. "Dear Mrs. Pizzella," the missive stated, "I regret the circumstances which require me to send you this note. Your son is a well-behaved boy and I enjoy having him as one of my students, but, unfortunately, in his academic skills, he is having difficulty keeping up with the rest of his class. Unless there is a drastic improvement in his grades between now and the end of the school year, I will have no alternative but to hold him back. Sincerely, Miss Quayle."

I hadn't read it, but I instinctively knew the essence of its content and I was curious to see how my mother would react. At the same time, I was relieved that my father wasn't home. With his explosive temper, he would be difficult. Still, I had implicit confidence in my mother's maternal ability to control the situation.

Fortunately for me, neither my mother nor my teacher had any inkling as to one of the root causes of my apparent academic inertia. It wasn't a purely intellectual deficiency. The problem had aspects that were definitely physiological. Miss Quayle was vastly different from any other teacher I had ever previously encountered. She was singularly gorgeous. Blond, blue-eyed and statuesque, she had a figure to die for. She was in her early twenties and had just married an airforce pilot. She was the first woman I ever noticed in this peculiar way and I couldn't get my eyes off her. Every part of her anatomy was perfectly proportioned and, when she moved, incomprehensible things happened inside of me. I was enveloped in a tidal wave of dulcet, symphonic strains. She stimulated glands which, heretofore latent, now mysteriously erupted, producing unfamiliar emotions and feelings which were as inexplicable and uncontrollable, as they were pleasurable and erratic. It would be premature to use the term "erotic." It wasn't until years later that I would fully comprehend those incipient flashes of eroticism.

It was one of the customs in those days to require those who performed poorly, in an academic sense, to sit at the

front of the class. What a delightful method of castigation! I
was always in the front row. It was also a custom to chastise
such laggards by compelling them to stay after school. Voila,
another punitive delight! I was frequently held after school.
And though I just couldn't seem to master my lessons, there
was no disputing the fact that I was extremely attentive. I
would offer to help her carry things to her car, as we left the
building together. I was so well behaved that my demeanor
assumed the appearance of innocence and, to this day, the
prurient feelings evoked by her proximity remain a deep, dark
secret. Thank God!

Mother calmly read the note, then paused and asked
me to sit down at the table. We were alone in the kitchen
and the table stood at the end of the room in front of a large
window that looked out into the backyard. I remember the
sun dancing gleefully on the table, as we sat down. She did
most of the talking, while I did some very attentive listening.
Knowing her aspirations, I was aware that I had let her
down and I felt wounded, guilty and ashamed. I waited for
her to get angry, so that I could become defensive and feel
justified in retaliation. I had dashed her hopes. I had hurt her.
Why wasn't she getting angry? Was she trying to trick me?
It wasn't supposed to work this way. She was supposed to
reprimand me, threaten to tell my father and then punish me.
This would permit me to cry and wallow in self-pity. All of this
would consume so much energy that we could both postpone
dealing with the problem.

In a very subtle way, she had turned the tables on me.
She was so gentle and understanding that I was forced to
listen and address my failures. I felt a void in the pit of my
stomach, an insatiable hunger to atone. I was irresistibly
impelled to correct my errant ways. I felt like I had climbed a
mountain and there, at the very top, paused to take a deep
breath and the air was so fresh and invigorating that I became
lightheaded. A crushing weight had been removed from my
chest. Suddenly, my ears were unblocked and my entire
being was permeated with the inspiring sound of her loving,
yet concerned voice. The hitherto locked compartments of my
brain flew open and the gray, spongy material within avidly

sucked up all of her pertinent and irrefutable revelations. I don't remember the specifics, but she was talking about the marvels of this great country, about the incredible opportunities available to kids like me to obtain an education, to acquire a profession, to make a good living and to become a responsible citizen. She spoke about her love for me, about how hard she and my father had to work to provide a home for me and my siblings, about how difficult it was for immigrants to survive in a strange new world and about my responsibilities as the offspring of immigrant parents. We must have talked for a couple of hours, but it seemed like this all took place in the blink of an eye.

The sun had set. It was dusk and, on that day, I instinctively knew that something very bizarre had taken place. I can't recall any particular words, or any agreement or plan of action or resolution, but, at the conclusion of that conversation, I was a totally different person. There was no doubt about it, a metamorphosis had occurred. I was no longer floundering in my attitude toward my studies. I knew precisely what I must do and had not the slightest doubt that I would attain my newly established goals. The gauntlet had been cast, the challenge accepted and naught was left but the duel.

When my mother spoke of hardship and what it took to make a home, I knew exactly what she meant. My father was a barber and she was a seamstress. With their combined incomes, we barely reached the poverty level, but they were blessed with magnificent energy, resourcefulness and pride. The word "welfare" was a profanity. No work was too demeaning and no recompense too meager. They were indefatigable.

(L-R) Louis, Ed and Mary Pizzella, ca 1950. Ed was in high school.

My father operated the Strand Barber Shop on Main Street, just north of Talcott Street in downtown Hartford. It was located across the street from the Strand Theater and next door to the Mohegan Market in the Pilgard Building. Every Sunday afternoon my father took me with him to clean the shop. My job was to mop the white ceramic tile floor and clean out the brass spittoons.

At home, one day a week was set aside to do all the clothes washing. This was done in the bathtub with a washboard and a manual wringer. Another day was set aside for baking. My mother would knead a mound of dough and then parcel it out into bread pans. She'd put the pans on the beds and cover them with blankets to allow the dough to rise. We would put up all our own canned goods. Whenever a particular fruit or vegetable was in season, my parents would buy several bushels and I would help my mother prepare the preserves and fill the Mason jars. And every fall, I'd help my father make the wine. He kept the crusher, the press and several wooden barrels in the basement. When harvest time came around, he would take me to the farmers' market on the

Boulevard and purchase a couple of dozen crates of grapes. He would open the crates and my job was to feed the grapes into the crusher, as I cranked the handle. I'll never forget the sweet, fruity taste of those plump, juicy globules. Needless to say, more than a negligible portion of the succulent contents of those containers never made its way into the mash.

Mother used to take me with her to the farmers' market, when she bought chickens. Those were the days before supermarkets, before pre-packaged frozen foods, before barcodes and price tags. She would barter enthusiastically with the farmer and, when the deal was struck, he'd shove three or four squawking hens into a burlap bag, which I'd sling over my shoulder and carry home. At that time, we were living on the fourth floor of a brick tenement house on the corner of Talcott and Market Streets. Our apartment overlooked St. Anthony's, a basement church. We'd take one of the chickens out for supper and put the others in a strawberry crate on the roof. I would go up there every day and feed them corn kernels until we required their services. You see, we had to be very selective about what we put in the icebox because it contained so little storage space.

I was certain that I could succeed academically, if I put my mind to it. As the result of economic necessity, I had already developed some attributes that would be extremely helpful. My father was only five feet tall and, when I was in the fourth grade, I was as tall as he. Since my parents couldn't afford to buy me clothes, I wore my father's hand-me-downs. My mother would alter his worn double-breasted, pin-striped suits and I would wear them to school. That's when I discovered the cruelty of my classmates. I became painfully aware that kids enjoyed picking out oddballs and teasing them mercilessly. Their objective was to provoke anger, which would then justify physical confrontation. Without anger on the part of the victim, the cycle was broken. I learned how to control my responses. This is the technique I would now employ in defense of my new persona. If I was to become a "grind," which is what they called guys who took books home from school, then I must prepare myself for the inevitable and relentless abuse that was sure to result from such deviant behavior.

When the heart-to-heart with my mother ended, we both knew the problem had been resolved. From that point on my grades were A's and B's and I made the honor roll every semester thereafter. I encountered an abundance of razzing, but I managed to roll with the punches and was never deterred from the accomplishment of my academic goals.

I turned to Marge and said, "I'll do it." Those words signaled the inception of my theatrical exploration, a delightful flight of fantasy on a magical carpet that, in the context of more than a hundred different theatrical settings spanning more than three decades, would in various dimensions of time propel me to the most exotic places on earth. In hindsight, I would compare the commencement of this odyssey to the moment when Dorothy, having miraculously survived the tornado's ferocity, cautiously opens the door of her gray, colorless existence to embrace the vivid hues of Munchkin Land and embarks on her adventurous journey over the serpentine yellow brick road in search of the Wizard of Oz.

I didn't realize it at the time, but I had been ideally prepared for this endeavor. Without trepidation or embarrassment, I had learned at an early age to don apparel that was guarantied to provoke the derisive laughter of my incredulous peers. Bringing home books—my classmates joked that I needed a wheelbarrow—and studying while my macho friends were hanging out on street corners, I had learned to temper my reactions to the boundless ridicule that would inevitably ensue and to which I had voluntarily subjected myself.

I had read and studied diligently and learned the niceties of language. I had learned how to express myself with intensity and clarity. I had forced myself tediously to memorize. In my oratorical exploits—as a ninth grader I had won my Junior High School's oratorical contest—and in my recitations in English class, I had learned to stand before an audience and recite with eloquence and passion. I had learned how to cast aside my inhibitions.

Often, while preparing for an entrance in my later theatrical endeavors, I would replay in the deep recesses of my mind my experiences in Miss Hoye's English class.

She had an infectious passion for poetry and often had us memorize her favorite pieces. Then she would call us up to the front of the class and exhort us to recite with feeling. I remember when she called on me to recite "High Flight" by John Gillespie Magee, Jr. I was determined to impress her and, with an authoritative voice which I drew up from the depths of my diaphragm, I flamboyantly recited that prophetic poem, which ironically depicted, not only my performance at that moment, but the emotions that I would repeatedly experience in my future escapades as a thespian. "Oh, I have slipped the surly bonds of earth and danced the skies on laughter-silvered wings. Sunward I've climbed and joined the tumbling mirth of sun-split clouds—and done a hundred things you have not dreamed of."

I went on to perform that bit part with the dynamic energy and unmitigated zeal that would normally be attributed to a major role. I had been blessed with a knack for languages and a perceptive ear. In my early years I spoke only Italian. My father had come to this country in his late teens. It took him a decade to establish his business and save enough money to return to his fatherland and visit his family. While there, he married my mother and a year later I was born in Hartford, Connecticut.

At the time of her arrival in this country, mother spoke not a word of English, so I spent my formative years speaking her native tongue. I attended the Brown Elementary School on Morgan Street, subsequently the home of the Hartford Police Department. In the first grade, I was fortunate to have a teacher with an Italian heritage. Miss Musio was bilingual and one of the few people with whom I was able to converse. Because of my language problem, I became her pet. She'd have me sit on the piano bench next to her whenever she held a sing-along.

Mother and I soon became fluent in English, but my experience with a foreign language provided me with a linguistic foundation which I effectively employed in many subsequent theatrical roles. In contrast to the actor I had replaced, I performed the role of John Fitzgerald with an Irish brogue, which added immeasurably both to its humor, as well as to the credibility of my characterization. This was my first exposure to the demands of comic timing. I'll never forget the exhilaration and feeling of power I experienced when I realized that, with proper rhythm, punctuation and projection, I could elicit laughter, applause and a gamut of emotional responses from people who were utter strangers. I had never taken drugs, but now I knew what a "high" must be like. I was addicted.

CHAPTER TWO

THE AWAKENING

"Come on Marge! Let's move it," I urged, tugging at her arm with unrestrained exuberance. My normally responsive wife was pensively hesitant. "Do you really think we should? We open in two weeks, you know," she replied with a hint of trepidation in her voice. "I'm a big boy and, besides, it's not my debut," I retorted tenaciously. "Your debut was all of five months ago," she laughed. "Anyway, it could affect your performance, couldn't it? It might induce you to change things and Moe would go into orbit." This was her one-two punch.

Although I disagreed with her, I could understand her hesitancy. She was catering to one of the oldest theatre taboos. After all, she was president of the local theatre group and, in that position, I suppose she was expected to observe all of the archaic, unwritten rules, one of which was that you never go to see someone else's version of a play you're about to stage. The reason behind the rule is obvious. Every director's interpretation of a script is, to some degree, unique and, since theatre is the most rigid of autocracies, an actor's exposure to another director's vision might engender equivocation, insecurity, confusion or deviation, deliberate or inadvertent, or even out and out insubordination. Although some actors might be vulnerable to such pitfalls, I felt immune because, even though it was early in my acting career, I had already begun to develop a high degree of independence and self-assurance and an insight rare among neophytes. When I perused a script, I read between the lines, literally, figuratively and imaginatively. I could actually visualize the action. It was as though I were watching a movie flashing across a tiny screen inside my head. As a consequence, in most of my later theatrical endeavors I required little direction. This creative knack proved to be immeasurably beneficial, especially when I turned my attention to directing.

Marge and Ed Pizzella

We had good seats. Whenever we went to a movie, Marge would insist that we sit two-thirds of the way back, so that everything would be in "proper perspective." She always said she got headaches from sitting too close to the screen, but, this time, kicking and screaming, I virtually dragged her down front. I wanted to be in a position to focus on every intricate move, every expressive intonation, every pregnant pause, every nuance of facial expression. After all, this was a first. I had been to hundreds of movies before, but never to one like this.

We waited anxiously for what we thought would be shear revelation. Patiently we tolerated the introductory and somewhat facetious admonitions about smoking and talking out loud in the theater. They seemed to me to be both demeaning and incongruous. I like to think that, if I wanted to smoke and talk out loud, I would have had the common decency to go to a bar, instead of a movie theater. I started to get edgy during the utterly superfluous directions to the fire exits which, of course, were unmistakably marked by brightly illuminated signs. I began to fume during the sophomoric pitch promoting the junk food concessions which, like indomitable hurdles, bombastically thwarted our entrance to the theater. And, finally, when the coming attractions were displayed, I was ready to explode. At last, the main feature started. Relieved, I sat back in my seat and, like a massive sponge, readied myself for illuminating, though passive, absorption. Did I say "passive?" Every time Paul Ford was about to utter a word, I would scream out the line. People turned in their seats and grimaced, while Marge shushed me in embarrassment, as she apologized to our distraught neighbors.

I was amazed by the coincidence. I thought it must be some kind of omen. Here, we had been rehearsing the stage play for about six weeks and, coincidentally, the celluloid version was playing at the local movie theater. Remember, this was in those primeval days before the advent of videotape players and Blockbuster's. And adding to my excitement was the fact that the leading male role, the role I would be playing on stage, was being portrayed by one of my favorite character actors. I had absolutely adored Paul Ford's characterization of the gullible, fumbling colonel in the Ernie Bilco television series.

Halfway into the story, it hit me like a ton of bricks. This movie, which I had anticipated with such anxiety, hoping it would give me valuable insights into the role I was about to portray, was flat and two dimensional. The pace was torturously slow and draggy. The comic lines, crisp on stage, here had no punch to them. There was no snap, no rhythm, no interplay with the audience. It was a dismal disappointment of epic proportions. Don't misunderstand me. The movie was good, as movies go, but comparing it to our exhilarating rehearsals and, therefore, my expectation of what the final product would be, I arrived at the undeniable conclusion that, as far as the film version was concerned, it was eons too late for "Never Too Late." It was at that moment that I came to recognize the distinct vitality of live theatre. This traumatic experience laid the foundation for my irresistible attraction to the stage with its challenging third dimension.

The disappointment compelled me to mentally retrace my steps and, in my subconscious, I reviewed the dynamics of our rehearsals. My wife was being played by Lavon Lach. Her husband, Walt, was an old friend of mine, a lawyer, who lived in Newington and had his office on Main Street in Hartford, across from City Hall, where I was working as a legal aid attorney. Walt and Lavon were active with Theatre Newington and had invited us to see "My Three Angels," where we met several members of the group. My son-in-law was being played by Howie Rosenthal, an extremely interesting character, on and off stage. I shivered every time I recalled the unbridled energy that nearly always prevailed from start to finish. So invigorating was the process that its mere anticipation virtually wafted me up the three flights of stairs of the old Town Hall. Back in those days, the municipal offices were located in the old Grange Hall on Main Street. It was a boxy, red brick three-story building with government offices on the first two floors and the Town Court on the third floor. At the top of the stairs, a large double door opened into an expansive room with a shiny oak floor and furnished with heavy, straight-backed oak chairs, a couple of rectangular oak tables and a mammoth, ornate oak desk, which sat on a platform to one side. Ironically, the use of the room alternated from judicial to theatrical, with the conversion being accomplished merely by the placement of the tables and chairs.

Theatre, of course, demands immense concentration, especially when you're on stage. But when you're backstage waiting for your cue, either during a rehearsal or a performance, the intensity occasionally diminishes and some are inclined to become bored or even doze. I've heard directors tell actors to bring along a book or magazine to prevent boredom from maturing either to malaise or disruption. I could never understand this. I've always managed to keep myself busy, either reviewing my lines or trying to perfect my blocking, my timing or my delivery. I must confess, however, that there were a few instances, when rehearsals became tedious, plodding or repetitious and I would lapse into a momentary daydream. When this occurred, I would inevitably focus on that monumental desk with its thick-set legs, ornately carved and bowed, not by design, I imagined, but in testament to their ponderous burden.

Gazing at that elaborate, gargantuan creation, it was easy to see why in ancient times it came to be identified with the omnipresent, overbearing authority of government. Like the sprawling agencies of authoritarian institutions, it too was bureaucratic. I would picture one of its robust ancestors pompously perched in some august chamber of the Tower of London in the reign of Henry VIII, or, better still, in a sultry dungeon hidden deep within the bowels of the formidable Bastille in those tempestuous days following the French Revolution.

Awkwardly propped behind it, and protected by its haughty prominence, would be a newly appointed magistrate of the Revolutionary Council, a boorish French peasant ominously wielding a heavy wooden gavel. Before it, intimidated by its arrogant, looming mass, would be an endless line of trembling French nobility, their faces grimly twisted with tense and fearful expressions indicative of the gravity of the proceedings. The solemn line, in the overpowering shadow of that menacing, impenetrable and unforgiving fortress of authority, would catatonically creep and jerk to the beat of the rhythmic dirge emitted by the resonant top of that behemoth desk, as that lethal gavel methodically struck, producing at first the deafening report of a cannon, then ironically trailing off in a whimpering death rattle.

I often thought that the talented craftsman, who fashioned that titanic masterpiece, must have done so right there on the third floor of the Town Hall, because it was much too massive to get up those three, steep flights of stairs.

Perhaps the reason I focused on that immense desk was that I was one of the few people who had become familiar with this room in two entirely different contexts. This place was an integral part of both my vocation and my avocation. It was years later when I would fully appreciate the overlapping similarities between the two. I would come to realize that the talents I developed in one could be effectively applied to the other with surprisingly beneficial results. I would especially marvel at how I could employ my ability as an actor to gratify a client, even in a losing case.

I'll never forget the first time I laid eyes on that awesome wooden monument. It was 1960, about a year after my young family and I had moved to Newington. I had just left my position as Assistant Legal Aid Attorney to become an associate in the Hartford law firm of Schatz & Schatz. I was now engaged in private practice and was anxious to broaden my experience. I had become acquainted with Judge Waldemar Lach, an attorney who lived in Newington, but practiced in Hartford. His office was across the street from City Hall, where my office was located, when I was with Legal Aid. Parking in the city was a problem, so we frequently rode together on the bus.

Walt had been active with the local Democratic Party and, after losing an election for state representative, managed to get himself appointed a municipal judge. Those were the days of the town courts, which held night sessions and thus effectively employed the after-hour talents of the local citizenry to inexpensively and expeditiously dispose of a plethora of minor civil and criminal cases. Amazingly, many of the judges and prosecutors were not even lawyers.

When I first passed the bar, blinded by idealism and intoxicated with my own self-importance, even the mention of a lay judiciary would have made my skin crawl. After more than fifty years of practice and having witnessed the moral devastation heralded by a professional, liberal, pro-active judiciary, however, I wonder if that system should not have been retained.

Walt and I had many interesting experiences riding to work together on the bus. I remember the events that occurred when he and his wife, Lavon, were planning a trip to Italy. He spoke no Italian and, recognizing that I was familiar with the language, he prevailed upon me to tutor him during our morning sojourns to the city. I would bring along my Italian grammar book and, on boarding the bus, we would go directly to the rear, where there were few passengers. After we settled down, I would coach him in Italian grammar, pronunciation and vocabulary. The lessons invariably started in an inaudible hush, but, as they progressed, grew louder and louder until the passengers in front turned around and burst into laughter.

Walt and his wife were members of Theatre Newington, the local community theatre group. They invited Marge and me to attend TN's production of "My Three Angels." We were so impressed that we joined and it wasn't long after that that Marge was elected President and I was appointed Business Manager.

It was through Walt that I had met Tony Palombizio, who operated an automotive repair business on the Berlin Turnpike. Tony was a truly unusual character. He was a successful and astute businessman, but you'd never know it to look at or talk to him. His manner was crude and burley and his diction was unmistakably that of a mobster. His nefarious demeanor was so convincing that he had been cast as an extra in the first two "Godfather" films. At the slightest provocation, he would display a photo taken on the movie set, which depicted him posed with a group of "good-fellows," holding a shotgun and standing with one foot casually propped on the running board of a vintage roadster.

This man derived ecstatic pleasure from intimidating people. I was young and somewhat naïve, so it took me a while to figure him out. At first, tucking my tail between my legs, I sheepishly cowered under the thrusts of his abrupt barbs, but later I learned that he enjoyed your company even more, if you returned insult for insult. I learned that beneath that contrived, course exterior lay a vast reservoir of sensitivity and compassion.

He knew I was a struggling young lawyer and offered to refer clients to me. One day, I received a telephone call from a prospective client, who said he'd been referred by Tony. He had been in an automobile accident and his car had been towed to Tony's garage for repair. He had been arrested for driving under the influence and asked me to defend him. I agreed to take the case. It would be my first DWI (driving while intoxicated) and my first case in the Newington Town Court.

I immediately obtained a copy of my client's motor vehicle record and found, to my dismay, that he had a recent DWI conviction. This raised the stakes, for a conviction on a second offense would surely have resulted in a jail sentence. I began to search desperately for a flaw in the prosecution's case. I looked for irregularities in the administration of the sobriety test, but there were none. The toxicology report indicated a reading substantially higher than the statutory limit. I was relentless in my quest for a defense, in order that I might build a favorable reputation and thereby encourage more referrals.

I reviewed the facts leading up to the accident. It had occurred on a weekend after two o'clock in the morning. My client had just left a bar and was driving home alone. He was headed south on the Berlin Turnpike. As he attempted to make a right-hand turn onto Robbins Avenue, because of his intoxicated condition, he was unable to properly negotiate the turn and mounted an embankment on the left-hand side of the road near McDonald's. When he became aware of the fact that he was off the pavement, he over-corrected by veering sharply to the right and abruptly ended up on the front porch of a house on the north side of Robbins Avenue.

The impact disengaged the veranda's supporting columns and its roof came tumbling down on top of the car. Fortunately, my client was uninjured and had the presence of mind to turn off the engine. When the police arrived, sometime later, they found him asleep in the driver's seat. The woman who lived in the house stated that she had been awakened by the sound of what she thought was one of her children falling out of bed. After she went to check the children and found them undisturbed, she came downstairs and, to her amazement, discovered my client asleep in his car on her front porch with the motor turned off. I had found my defense.

The night my case was scheduled, I energetically scaled the three steep flights to the third floor courtroom. Although I was a little winded, I immediately focused on that massive, intimidating symbol of authority. I was so mesmerized by the power it projected that it was not until my case was called that I realized that Judge Lach was sitting. He was a tall, overpowering man, but behind that monstrous desk he looked like a midget.

Buoyed by what I thought would be a friendly reception, I smugly entered a plea of not guilty. With furrowed brow, he sternly looked down at me. He reminded me of a supercilious Indian handler, seated atop his pachyderm, who might at any random moment signal his obedient, omnipotent beast to whimsically crush me like an egg.

I felt a little woozy, as I timidly handed him my motion for dismissal, together with a supporting memorandum of law. In those exculpatory documents I had quoted the language of the drunk driving statute and argued that my motion should be granted on the ground that the State could not prove the essential element of operation. He quickly scanned the paperwork and then turned to the prosecutor and asked if he had any witnesses, who could establish that the accused had been operating the vehicle, as required by the statute. There was a momentary pause as the prosecutor, whom I later learned was Bruno Perlini, reviewed his file.

Bruno was not a lawyer. He was a local businessman, who made his living as a distributor of Stella D'Oro cookies. He had been appointed to this position through his involvement with the local Democratic Party. Years later, I served with him on the Newington Town Council and found him to be quite affable, despite the somewhat aloof demeanor he had displayed in his prosecutorial role. My heart began to palpitate, as I waited for that hostile wooden monster to open up and swallow me. When the prosecutor responded in the negative, the judge slammed down his gavel and reluctantly grunted, "Dismissed." I think I was the only one present who detected a glint in the judge's eye.

Ironically, I later learned that the front porch, which had been summarily amputated by my inebriated client, could not be reconstructed because the house predated the establishment of building setback lines and was too close to the street.

Marge and I had come to see this movie out of curiosity. You might call it an experiment. I was anxiously anticipating the opening of a play in which I would be performing my first leading role and I wanted to learn as much as I could about the mechanics of creating empathy. I was intrigued with the idea of comparing two very different modes of communicating with an audience. It was not until I had stepped on stage in the role of an Irish tax collector that I began to recognize the distinction between the two art forms. Viewing this film clearly exposed that distinction. It was my awakening.

CHAPTER THREE

SEDENTARY THESPIANS

As we watched the film, interrupted by the occasional annoyance of mumbled lines blurted sporadically through my embarrassed wife's tightly clasped fingers defensively cupped over my insurgent mouth, I couldn't help but think of how, piece by piece, over six weeks of intense rehearsals, we had succeeded in constructing a vibrant, three dimensional stage version of the rather flat and uninspiring representation we were presently viewing. And it was in those highly charged and disciplined rehearsals that, step by step, I was learning the essentials of what was to become a demanding, yet irresistible avocation. I found myself peculiarly suited to this endeavor. After all, I was adept at memorizing and oratory. What other skills would be required?

It was dress rehearsal and I had been admonished about not allowing any "white spaces," or gaps in dialogue. Each actor, I was told, must start speaking on the last word of the cue or prior line. Only in special circumstances, such as situations where emphasis is required, was even a split second of silence tolerated. We were at the point in the rehearsal where the family had gathered for a serious discussion. The scene builds to a climax, when Lavon is supposed the make an abrupt and unexpected entrance, which immediately creates a deafening silence. Well, Lavon was having trouble with a costume change and missed her entrance. I immediately started adlibbing to cover. The other actors joined me and we continued making up dialogue for what seemed an eternity, until she finally appeared.

Never Too Late in rehearsal

"Never Too Late"—(L-R) Carole Sneideman, Lavon Lach, Ed Pizzella and Howie Rosenthal.

It was then that I was first struck with the theatrical importance, nay the indispensability, of chairs. In "Suds In Your Eye," I had been deprived of the total picture. I came in at the last minute. When I joined the cast in that production, the actors were already rehearsing on the completed set. Having acted as the group's business manager, I was remotely familiar with the initial stages of a production, but I had never directly experienced rehearsing with chairs, i.e. before the set was constructed and in place. Until now, I did not realize that, of the vast variety of inert tangible objects that would be employed in the completion of our theatrical venture, it was these unpretentious and unobtrusive furnishings that would make the greatest contribution.

"Never Too Late"—(L-R) Art Favreau (the Doctor) Ed Pizzella and Lavon Lach.

At each rehearsal, the first and perhaps most important chore, which had to be performed before we could start, was for the actors to methodically arrange the chairs to form a crude representation of what would eventually be the set. Innocently, those oaken pawns retained their simple, unbeguiling appearance and customary function up to the moment they were put in place. At that very instant, as if they had somehow become the magical props of David Copperfield, they were inexplicably transformed into doors, windows, tables, sofas, stairways, walls and a myriad of other structures, fixtures and furnishings essential to the environment and action of the play. And each member of the cast, focusing upon his or her blocking or the delivery of his or her lines, instinctively accorded profound credibility to the powerful sedentary performance of those lifeless imposters.

To any unsuspecting, non-theatrical person, who might casually walk in during a rehearsal, these commonplace, unremarkable furnishings would obviously retain their normal appearance, their peculiar arrangement not being suggestive of any functional transformation. But a thespian, though not being familiar with the play or with the precise contextual significance of these otherwise ordinary fixtures, would immediately detect that a mystical metamorphosis had occurred. Years later, I would memorialize this phenomenon in poetic form. Thus I wrote:

CHAIRS

In all my days, I've never viewed
A thing so bountifully imbued
As that on which I sit my seat,
Whose praises I shall now repeat.

Most humble of all furnishings,
Hard of surface or with springs,
Chairs are found where folks recline,
At home, at work and where they dine.

As though by Nightingale inspired,
Supporting those infirm or tired,
Who, other than a lowly chair,
Exhibits such concern and care?

Though often blank in their expression,
Chairs, too, are subject to depression,
For, like us folks, who troubles share,
Heavy burdens do they bear.

They neither court, nor do they marry
And, though their life is sedentary,
For themselves they've made a niche;
Beloved are they by poor and rich.

I've found, if chairs are not abused,
With loyalty they seem infused
And this is why they've gained renown,
As seldom prone to let one down.

No bias do they e'er display,
Embracing all who come their way
And, though they hold us up at times,
They've ne'er committed any crimes.

Their sheer simplicity beguiles,
But having walked for several miles,
The ambler's pleased to find a chair,
To which he hastens to repair.

I'd buy their stock without delay,
For chairs, I'll vow, are here to stay.
Invulnerable to changing trends,
They neatly gather up loose ends.

Of plastic, metal or of wood,
A chair has in its life withstood
A sum of weight one cannot measure,
Sedately bearing loads of leisure.

Chairs cater not to folks high born,
But offer rest to those forlorn.
Though they may be devoid of wit,
On them both weak and mighty sit.

The functions of a chair are clear
And it performs them without peer.
Though to sloth it may incline,
It yet attends the bottom line.

The beans I'm here quite apt to spill,
For though it does its work with skill,
In its endeavors bear in mind
That it will often get behind.

Enticing though the baker's trade,
In view of all the dough he's made,
If shapely buns should pull you chain,
Imagine all that chairs contain.

Appearing passive and inert,
It yet wields power to assert,
For, lacking inspirational gifts,
It still persistently uplifts.

It's something every king must own,
Though in this context it's a throne;
And college management it shares,
For aren't department heads called chairs?

In corporations, thank the Lord,
The CEO oft chairs the board.
It's plain that chairs are not just grunts,
But capable of mighty stunts.

No object surely can compare,
In breath of usage, to a chair,
Whose sturdy limbs are firmly set
To hold a person, thing or pet.

As a ladder, stool or tabletop,
Their applications never stop.
These uses every day we spy,
But many more yet do apply.

Evading not the grueling chore,
With vigor did I then explore
And thus with confidence opine
Chairs far exceed their plain design.

To most a chair is just a seat,
But there are others you will meet
To whom a chair may represent
Each item in the firmament.

A theatre buff is one of these;
A chair is everything he sees.
Rehearsals start; the stage is bare,
So every set piece is a chair.

A chair's a window, couch or door,
A wall or stairs and even more;
A place or thing of every kind,
Whatever's in the playwright's mind.

Though elsewhere they are incidental,
In theatre chairs are fundamental.
With varied ids in their collection,
They never fail to take direction.

Unrestrained, unfettered, free,
A chair evokes diversity.
It whisks us off upon a trip,
Impersonating train or ship.

A vehicle it well could be;
Accouterments of royalty;
Antiques, equipment used in sport,
Contrivances of every sort.

No limits is it bound to heed
And therefore meets our every need.
Never ceasing to amaze,
One marvels at the roles it plays.

In this vain, a chair will test
The skills with which an actor's blessed,
His discipline and concentration
And, most of all, imagination.

With legs that neither run nor climb,
The chair's withstood the test of time.
The resting place of every sage,
This veteran never shows its age.

Armed with background so diverse,
If with chairs one might converse,
A wealth of knowledge would be told,
Derived from all the tales they hold.

Before an actor I became,
A chair to me was just the name
Of that on which I'd set my frame,
And not this star of broad acclaim.

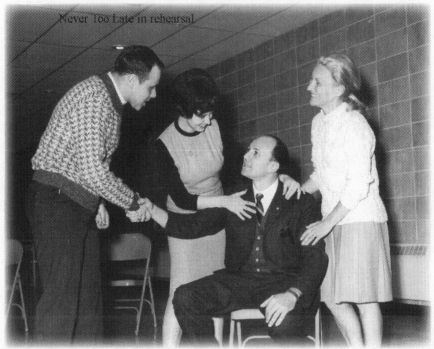

"Never Too Late"—(L-R) Howie Rosenthal, Carole Sneidman, Ed Pizzella and Lavon Lach in rehearsal at the Knights of Colombus Hall, No. Mountain Road.

Moe Smith was a man who, in a theatrical context, fully recognized the unparalleled versatility of chairs, as well as the extraordinary mischief that would certainly ensue from their inadvertent misplacement, or from the failure to accord them their assigned theatrical significance.

A huge, bellowing bear of a Swede, Moe enjoyed the position of being Theatre Newington's favorite director. He was truly outstanding. He was six and a half feet tall with an imposing head, piercing eyes, a voice like a foghorn and a prominent, square jaw that was unquestionably built to deliver the last word. When Moe looked at you, you couldn't help but be intimidated. The paradox was that, beneath that overbearing façade, he was compassionate, sensitive and gentle as a lamb. The deception was immediately exposed by a warm smile and a boisterous laugh that seemed to emanate from a bass drum concealed in the remote recesses of that massive frame. I'll never forget the time I heard that reverberating laugh in stereo.

"Never Too Late," the stage play, is a three-act comedy about the perplexing and sometimes humorous problems confronted by a middle-aged couple anticipating the arrival of a change-of-life baby. The undaunted duo bravely face up to the complexities resulting from the unintended pregnancy and must now make drastic and unexpected alterations in the previously comfortable pattern of their lives. They plan the addition of a nursery and Harry orders the building materials. Living directly across the street from the mayor, Harry is utterly humiliated when the delivery man leaves the toilet in plain view on the front lawn. Fearing that he will become the butt of his honor's renowned, sarcastic humor, he hurriedly removes it from the front lawn and temporarily deposits it in the living room. Now comes an intensely dramatic scene in which the family gathers in the living room for a serious discussion about the disruptive affects of the pregnancy on their lives.

In rehearsal, the toilet, as with all the other essential set furnishings, was represented by a chair. The scene builds to a climax in which Harry, lamenting his fate, delivers a highly dramatic monologue about his heretofore impeccable standing in the community and the catastrophic embarrassment this predicament has caused him and, at the pinnacle of his impassioned soliloquy, he is blocked to sit on the sofa, which, of course, is also represented by a chair.

The intensity builds to a peak, but instead of sitting on the chair representing the sofa, I mistakenly sat on the chair representing the toilet, which unexpectedly gives my line a double entendre and changes its impact from solely dramatic to dramatic punctuated by farce.

Suddenly the rehearsal is thrown into pandemonium, as an earth shattering rumble rocks the hall. Horrified, we stop in our tracks, as the deafening, undulating sound waves reverberate throughout the room. Instinctively, we all look over to where the director had been standing. Our amazement turns to panic, as our attention is drawn to Moe, frantically jerking, twisting and writhing on the floor in a fetal position.

The abrasive, sonic blast continues, as we huddle around him in alarm. He was convulsive with laughter. This must have been "the bellow heard 'round the world." When all the guffaws subsided, Moe wiped away his tears and said to me, "change your blocking and make sure you keep that bit in!" I did and, sure enough, it drew rollicking laughs, when the show opened at the Martin Kellogg auditorium.

Thus was the incredible versatility of chairs indelibly impressed in the hidden recesses of my blossoming theatrical psyche.

CHAPTER FOUR

SIMON SAYS

"The Odd Couple"—Ed Pizzella as Oscar Madison

I was well on my way, climbing the theatrical ladder. In two shows I had risen from a stand-in in a comic bit role to a Paul Ford type leading man. I was hooked. It was at this point that I first made the acquaintance of the renowned

Neil Simon, figuratively speaking, that is. Theatre Newington had decided to do "The Odd Couple." Howie Rosenthal is a unique character on and off stage. He had played the role of my son-in-law in "Never Too Late." In every respect, we were opposites, yet we got along famously. He was good-natured and naïve with a whiney, effeminate flare, while I was completely at home as a crusty, cantankerous and incorrigible slob. We had enjoyed working with each other in the prior show and, as fortune would have it, we auditioned and were cast as Oscar and Felix.

This was my first opportunity to work with a new director. Theatre Newington had engaged the services of the Hole In The Wall's celebrated Ray Shinn. With all his bluster, Ray knew everything there was to know about comedy and especially Neil Simon. But he was also a world apart from the courteous, considerate and tactful Moe Smith. Ray's bullying was notorious. New Britain's Hole In The Wall Theatre had acquired a reputation for its innovative and intimate, avant-garde productions and Ray was one of its illustrious founders. He was an irascible, sarcastic, abrupt, unpredictable, chain-smoking, beer-drinking and overbearing boor and, at the same time, brilliant, witty, eloquent and charming.

Director Ray Shinn

Ellen Lau was an attractive young woman, who had been cast in the role of one of the Pigeon sisters. She was an outstanding actress with an unbelievable resume and, in this show, she would be making her debut with Theatre Newington. During our rehearsals and in our frequent nightly encounters at various local watering holes, I had gotten to know Ray and had become accustomed to many of his offensive mannerisms. I took his harassment on stage as a compliment. Whenever he screamed profanities at me during rehearsals, I knew he was trying to make me a better actor. But Ellen didn't know him, like I did. She did not realize that his invectives were not malevolent. I remember one rehearsal when he brought her to tears. Knowing her vast experience, I was amazed and I was also worried that she might quit. She didn't and the show was extremely successful.

The Ed Pizzella family ca. 1970—(Back row) Rick, Steve and Ed.
(Front row) Laura, Marge, Linda and Mike.

Marge and the kids frequently helped with my lines and sometimes they knew them and the blocking and comic bits as well as I did. It was in this show that I received my most demonstrative lessons in pacing and comic timing.

Felix decides to flaunt his culinary skills and comes out of the kitchen with a plate of steaming pasta. As he and his roommate argue back and forth, Oscar refers to it as "spaghetti." Felix looks at him in disgust and says, "It's not spaghetti, it's linguine." Oscar then sprays it with insecticide, picks up the plate and throws it into the kitchen, saying, "Now it's garbage!" Although this is supposed to be a big laugh line, my efforts were rewarded with little more than a twitter. I was mortified. When the curtain came down, I worked on my timing. I was determined to get the laugh this line was designed to evoke. I remembered what Moe Smith and Ray Shinn had said about the importance of the comic beat. I reworked my timing and the next night got thunderous laughter.

One night my five year old daughter, Linda, was sitting in the front row. She had seen and heard me rehearsing my lines at home on many occasions. When I picked up the plate of pasta, she got up and, turning to the audience, announced, "He's going to throw it into the kitchen!" Her timing was perfect and, needless to say, she's the one who got the big laugh that night.

I was thrilled with the author's hilarious one-liners and his brilliant comedic design. I marveled at how in the first two acts he could so intricately construct the characters and the story line that, in the opening five minutes of the third act, he evokes a stream of uncontrollable laughter without a word being spoken. This is true genius. And yet much is also left to the artistic skill of the director. He must appropriately interpret and orchestrate. He must convert the two dimensional, written word to three dimensional action. This is when I first fully recognized the creative marvel of live theatre. I was awed by the ability of a director and his cast to breathe life into the written word.

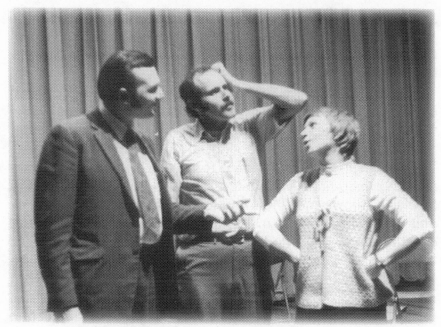

"The Odd Couple"—Ed Pizzella, as Oscar, Howie Rosenthal, as Felix, and Ellen Lau, as one of the Pigeon sisters.

"The Odd Couple" was one of the most successful productions in the history of TN and I was immensely elated by the review that appeared in the November 26, 1970 issue of the local newspaper, the Newington Town Crier: "Ed Pizzella, as the crude, course, but lovable Oscar Madison, was the backbone of the play. His complete command of lines and vocal modulation of their delivery were only part of a steady, workmanlike performance that actually held the play together."

I was driven to learn more. Marge and I had seen "The Impossible Years" on Broadway starring Lou Jacoby in the role of Dr. Jack Kingsley. I laughed so hard it hurt. We proposed that TN do the show and the group agreed. Again, I was cast in the lead role. Though not Neil Simon, it too was a hilarious comedy. The story line involves a know-it-all psychiatrist, the father of two teenaged daughters, who is writing a book about how to effectively handle the problems that inevitably arise in the course of parenting such unpredictable female offspring. Every time he completes a chapter in which he calmly and masterfully resolves the problem on which it focuses, the identical situation occurs in real life and, driven to distraction, he manifests utter incompetence.

It was in this show that I learned that I could do things on stage that I could never do in real life. In one scene, while my wife and I are out, my daughters, without our knowledge, have invited a group of teenagers to a party at our home. We return unexpectedly, only to be greeted by a raucous mêlée of inebriated youngsters. When I confront one of the boys, he throws me a left hook which sends me into the air and then backward on my butt. This is where I learned that on stage the action is reversed. In real life it's the force of the assailant's attack that propels the victim. On stage, the victim anticipates the thrust and propels himself. I practiced my reaction to the left hook, but I forgot to take my wallet out of my back pocket. Needless to say, proof that I had rehearsed came in the form of bruises on my right buttock. But it worked and the audience was convinced that I had been decked.

I also learned how to portray myself as being hung-over. In the play, my daughters literally drive me to drink and one of the acts ends with my getting wasted. The following act opens the next morning, as I make my entrance, coming down a flight of stairs from my bedroom, tormented by a devastating hangover. Waiting backstage for my cue, I would put myself into a trance, simulating a drunken stupor with its well-known resulting consequences.

While I was in my own little world psyching myself in preparation for my entrance, out of the corner of my eye I would see other members of the cast glaring at me, as though I were out of my mind. In particular, I remember the peculiar looks I received from Nancy Barnacle and Lou Grimaldi. This is how I earned the comment made by the reviewer in the Town Crier's issue of April 22, 1971: "The play's sparkle and celerity came only with extraordinary acting. Veteran actor Ed Pizzella, as the vocally explosive author-psychiatrist, purred, postured, pranced and pummeled his way to brilliant characterization." And this was only my fourth show. Years later the theatre group would look upon this season as one of the most successful in their entire existence.

In 1971, Newington celebrated its centennial anniversary. A local resident, Tom Atwater, had authored a pageant depicting the Town's early history. Sam Capuano directed and I was cast as two of the Town's founding fathers, Richard Beckley and Jabez Whittlesey. The pageant was produced at the new high school's auditorium. The things that impressed me most were the authentic costuming and the immensity of the theatre. The auditorium could seat eleven hundred.

"The Star Spangled Girl"—Ellen Lau, as Sophie Rauschmeyer and Ed Pizzella, as Andy Hobart.

The next season started with another Neil Simon comedy, "The Star-Spangled Girl" and I was again cast in a leading role. Howie Rosenthal was cast in the role of Norman Cornell, a comic character, and I was Andy Hobart, the straight man. We were fortunate to have Ellen Lau, who had played one of the Pidgeon sisters in "The Odd Couple" as Sophie Rauschmeyer. This show, I knew, was going to be very different because it was being directed by Al Fair, a theatre acquaintance of mine, who had never directed me, but whom I had seen on stage many times and who was well respected as an actor. In temperament, Al was the direct opposite of Ray Shinn. He knew comedy and was mild mannered with a rye sense of humor. I was looking forward to working with Howie and Ellen again.

Al Fair—Director of "The Star Spangled Girl."

One night, the director whispered to me that he would like to speak to me privately after rehearsal. I was then 39 years old and balding. He pulled me aside and said that he was pleased that I had agreed to take the role, but he was a little concerned because I looked somewhat older than the character depicted in the script. He asked if I would mind rejuvenating my appearance by wearing a toupee. This is when I was first struck with the essential importance of the character's appearance. Of course, I agreed. I immediately went to see my barber and friend, Louie Garzone. Lou was an amazing man. He was an Italian immigrant, who had come to this country as a young boy. My dad hired him and he worked in my father's barbershop until dad retired. At that point, he opened his own shop in Newington.

Lou obtained some hairpieces. I tried them on, selected one and Lou trimmed it to fit me. I wore it to the next rehearsal and the director was pleased. Not only was the director content with my newly altered appearance, but my wife, Marge, was also impressed and suggested that I wear it in my everyday life. I accepted the suggestion and wore it for a number of years thereafter. What's ironic is that my theatrical pursuits had induced me to don the toupee, but, after this show, I wore it continuously in real life and seldom on stage.

Fortunately, I knew something about this show and was boosted in my preparation to do it by a riveting experience that had occurred only a short time before. I had gone to see the Mark Twain Masquers' production of this show at the Wadsworth Atheneum in Hartford. It was directed by David Young. As the show opened, I was impressed by the quick pace and the tidal waves of laughter provoked by Neil Simon's brisk one-liners.

As the play continued, the laughs gradually diminished and the audience remained virtually silent until the final curtain. I was utterly baffled by the audience's lack of response and felt sympathy for the actors. At the opening, the laughter must have propelled them to an incredible high, only to be battered down time after time thereafter by devastating silence. I knew first hand what it was like to be standing on stage, waiting for the expected laugh that never came. It took me a minute to figure it out. The actors were not holding for laughs. If you don't hold after a laugh line, the audience is afraid to laugh for fear they will miss the next line.

In this show I began to develop my knack for adlibbing to cover a flub and I learned how a play can be enhanced by a director's use of imagination. Throughout the play the author alludes to characters, who are never seen on stage. There's dialogue about the landlady who rides a minibike and Sophie's boyfriend, a six foot Marine. The director decided to add a few laughs by having these characters appear in the curtain call. He recruited Beverly Sorber, who later became TN's President, as the landlady, and a Newington Police Officer, as the marine. His objective was accomplished, but one night we had a close call.

Near the end of the show, Howie handcuffs me to a steam pipe. A few moments later, he unlocks the cuffs and leaves in a huff. Then there's a blackout and, as part of the curtain call, the landlady enters and does a turn around the stage on her minibike. On this particular night, the pipe mysteriously falls down across the stage in front of the point where the landlady is shortly to make her entrance. Fearing that the landlady will fall over the pipe, I adlib a cue to Howie as he begins to exit, saying "And don't forget to take your damned steam pipe with you!" The audience screams, Howie takes the pipe offstage and the landlady is saved.

The November 16, 1971 issue of the New Britain Herald commented: "This fast moving comedy has but three characters. Ed Pizzella plays 'Andy Hobart,' Howard Rosenthal, 'Norman Cornell,' and Ellen Lau, 'Sophie Rauschmeyer,' a southern girl in the big city of San Francisco. All three actors kept the pace interesting and helped make the plot believable. Rosenthal, as a nervous writer, was outstanding, as was Pizzella, as the fast talking editor."

In 1972, Theatre Newington decided to establish a touring group that could be used to promote its major productions. This would be a portable one-act show that would be offered to local civic groups, as entertainment at their functions. Guess who was chosen to head the group. I took it upon myself to cast and direct a one-act play entitled "Three On A Bench." This was my first opportunity to direct and it exposed me to an entirely new facet of theatre. Betty Covey was one of my cast members and I played the role of Officer Callahan, which gave me the chance to revisit the Irish brogue that so embellished my stage debut. The set consisted of a bench placed in front of a free-standing painted cardboard backdrop. I had never before given any serious thought to directing, but this experience awakened me to another fascinating avenue for the development and exploitation of creativity in the theatrical venue.

"Three On A Bench"—Betty Covey and Ed Pizzella.

During my tenure as a member of the Town Council, we authorized the construction of a new high school on Willard Avenue and the conversion of the old high school on Cedar Street to a Town Hall, as a replacement for the antiquated facility in the old Grange Hall on Main Street. On April 14, 1972, the auditorium in the new Town Hall was officially dedicated as a Community Theatre facility and, as Theatre Newington President, my wife, Marge, participated in the ribbon-cutting ceremony with Mayor Elmer Mortensen and Town Manager Peter Curry.

Community Theatre Dedication: Mayor Mortensen, Marge Pizzella, TN President, Town Manager Peter Curry and the Assistant Town Manager.

Although I only played a supporting role in "Don't Drink The Water," as Ambassador McGee, I had the exhilarating pleasure of working with my radio idol, Charlie Parker. He was WDRC's station manager and possessed the most appealing resonant voice I have ever heard. He was also blessed with the most incredibly sharp wit and an infectious sense of humor. Whenever I was in his company, he would invariably cause my sides to ache and, when I was with him on stage, I found it extremely difficult to stay in character. No one has ever been able to tickle my risibles like Charlie.

Charlie Parker played leading roles in "Don't Drink The Water" and "Avanti."

Because of his many professional commitments, Charlie was not able to participate in very many of TN's productions, but on a number of occasions he graciously invited us to his studio, where he taped voice-overs and sound effects, which immeasurably enhanced many of TN's theatrical offerings. It was Charlie who introduced his son Steve to the magic of theatre and Steve worked as a techie on a number of TN productions. Steve handled the sound for "Don't Drink The Water" and this is how he looked then.

In 1973, Steve Parker handled sound for "Don't Drink The Water."

It's apparent that Steve inherited his keen wit and sense of humor from his talented dad. He followed in his father's footsteps and, in addition to the many hours he's donated to community access television, he has become a well-known local radio and TV personality. Witness his hilarious, fast-talking Bedding Barn commercials.

Radio and TV personality, Steve Parker.

The show was directed by the extremely talented Ted Guhl, a close friend of Ray Shinn and one of the Founders of the Hole In The Wall Theatre in New Britain, and I enjoyed working with him. Little did I know then that five years later I would have the pleasure of again working under his direction, but this time in one of my favorite leading roles, that of Emile Debecque in "South Pacific."

Ted Guhl, Director of "Don't Drink The Water."

At this point, I had completed my duties as Grand Knight of the Rev. Edward Shaughnessy Council Knights of Columbus and I had served two terms as a Republican member of the Newington Town Council. In my first term, I had had some disagreements with my party over the construction of a new Town Hall. The municipal offices were located in a small antiquated brick building on Main Street. No one disputed the fact that new facilities were needed. Because of the availability of state and federal grants for school construction, the then Republican Mayor, Elmer Mortensen, devised a plan to build a new eight million dollar high school on federally donated land on Willard Avenue and, at a cost of several more millions, to convert the old high school to a Town Hall. On the other hand, the Newington Children's Hospital offered to donate five acres of land on Constance Leigh Drive in the heart of the Town's business center for a new town hall. I had served as President of the Newington Chamber of Commerce and from the point of view of both location and cost, I thought that the latter plan was better and publicly argued for its adoption.

When I ran for re-election after my first term, I received the highest number of votes in the Town Council race, but because of my open disagreement with the Republican policy makers, I was denied the appointment of Deputy Mayor, which was traditionally conferred on the most popular majority party candidate. Further retaliation came when I was denied the nomination to run for a third term. The Republican caucus in which I was defeated, however, was rigged and I appealed to the Republican State Central Committee and won. State Central rejected the caucus nominations and ordered an open primary. This was the first time in Connecticut history that a local party caucus was overturned. Needless to say, because of the animosity I had aroused, I suffered a narrow loss in the primary and temporarily retired from local politics.

CHAPTER FIVE

THE PRISONER'S ESCAPE

"I'm Herbert"—Marge and Ed Pizzella

By 1974, I had done eleven shows, each of which continued to pique my theatrical curiosity and offered me the opportunity to hone my skills, the last three especially. They were notable because, in all three, I would share the lead with my theatrical mentor, my wife, Marge. This gave us the unique opportunity of rehearsing our lines at home. And two of the three shows, "You Know I Can't Hear You When The Water's Running" and "Critic's Choice," for me represented a completely novel and intriguing format. These were the first two major productions I had ever done in the round and in a dinner theatre setting. This was my first real taste of intimate theatre and I loved it.

"You Know I Can't Hear You When The Water's Running"—(Act II—"The Footsteps Of Doves") Ed Pizzella, as George, and Kay West, as Harriet.

There was a well-known restaurant on the Berlin Turnpike called the Matarese Circle. They had a large banquet hall in the basement. Theatre Newington entered into a joint venture agreement under which the theatre group would be responsible for the show and the restaurant would handle the food and the ticket price would be shared. The response was so favorable that I was reluctant to return to the old format.

What was most appealing about this format was that movements on stage were much more natural than those designed for the proscenium mode and, because of the intimacy, it was easier for me to develop a rapport with the audience. In one performance of "You Know I Can't Hear

You . . . ," when I was playing the role of George in the bedding store, I delivered an excruciating, long line and, by the time I was finished, I was so parched that I didn't think I could continue, so I reached over to a nearby table and snatched up what appeared to be a glass of water and gulped it down. It was a martini.

"The Footsteps Of Doves"—Ed Pizzella, as George, and Lynn Aune, as Jill.

The show was directed by Edith Zeldes and Marge Clauson, both long time members of TN. Edith later became theatre correspondent for the Newington Town Crier.

"You Know I Can't Hear You . . ."—Co-directors Edith Zeldes and Marge Clauson.

The thing that fascinated me about this show was the drastic change I had to make from the middle aged husband in the second act to the senile octogenarian in the third act. The change must have been convincing because we played to packed houses and the laughs were interminable. The show was so successful that we subsequently reproduced it at the Knights of Columbus Hall, as a joint political fundraiser for the two local political parties. I gave Charlie Casalengo the idea for the program's cover design and this is what he drew:

Program for joint political fundraiser.

In those days there was a bookstore at the easterly end of Market Square. Not long after we had closed, I saw a notice in the local paper that Robert Anderson, the play's author, had just published a novel and would be appearing at the bookstore for a signing. Marge and I decided to attend. We met Mr. Anderson and told him we had just done his show. He chuckled and proceeded to recount an episode that had occurred at its opening in London.

He prefaced the story by reminding us that the last act, "I'm Herbert," is written as dysfunctional or unrelated dialogue, that many of the lines are similar and are repeated and much of the humor arises from the fact that a statement, made by one of the pair, is denied by the other and a few moments later is repeated, as new information, by the one who had previously denied it. When the show opened in London, the stage hand responsible for drawing the curtain was given a line at the end of the act, as his cue to pull the curtain. As fate would have it, there was a line at the beginning of the act that was almost identical. It differed from the cue line by a couple of very common words. One of the actors inadvertently transposed the two lines and the curtain came down only minutes after the act opened.

I was always pleased with the compliments I received from members of the audience after the curtain calls, but there was one type of compliment that invariably caused me to chuckle. Every now and then a naïve admirer would come up to me and say, "I don't know how you were able to memorize all those lines!" Outwardly, I would try to appear gracious, but inside I'd say to myself, "Are you kidding? Memorizing the lines was the easy part!"

Considering such things as blocking, physical movement, characterization, speech patterns, facial expressions, projection, rhythm, intonation—the myriad of traits and functions that are essential to and must be appropriately blended to effectively flesh out a role—memorizing the lines is just the first of many steps in the actor's preparation. But in this case, memorizing the lines of one of the senile couple in the third act, was exceptionally difficult. The dialogue was so illogical, contradictory, repetitious and disjointed that it was virtually impossible to employ the customary, contextual associations that an actor normally relies on in the learning process. There was no alternative but to learn the lines by rote.

I learned another important lesson in preparing for this show: when something goes wrong—when something unexpected happens—you have to adlib or cover and, in the process, you have to play it up in an exaggerated manner. Al Fair, who directed me in "The Star-Spangled Girl" would explain that "The audience is very perceptive. They're focused on everything that happens on stage. When something unexpected occurs, they are immediately aware of it and if you ignore it, or try to sweep it under the rug, it makes them nervous. You've got to get them to loosen up and enjoy the show. And the only way you can do that is to highlight the flub and play it up big."

During the dress rehearsal, when I got up from my rocking chair and rested my hand on the back of the rocker, a decorative knob fell off and rolled onto the stage. Without the slightest hesitation and without interrupting my line, I went over to it, picked it up, stared at it and then casually popped it into the pocket of my sweater. The added bit drew a big laugh from the crew and the few spectators.

In 1974, Marge and I played the roles of the parents in "Time Out For Ginger." The leading role was played by Mellie Neiman, Joe Neiman's daughter, and Matt Zadrowski, Beverly St.Onge and Donna Grimaldi-Percoski played supporting roles. The play was directed by Frank Cammarata.

"Time Out For Ginger"—Donna Grimaldi, Marge Pizzella, Beverly St.Onge and Mellie Neiman. New Britain Herald photo, Nov.2, 1974.

When Theatre Newington's executive board announced that their next show would be "Critic's Choice," Marge and I were ecstatic, not only because of the storyline—the show centers about a theatre critic, who pans his actress-wife's show, but because it was to be produced as dinner theatre in the round at the Matarese Circle. Marge and I were again cast in the leading roles and our son was played by Attorney Mark Shipman's son. Intimate theatre was beginning to grow on me. This show also instilled in me the latent desire to perform the functions of a theatre critic, which desire was not satisfied until 1988, when I reviewed "The Rainmaker" and "Bell, Book And Candle" at the Hole In The Wall Theatre in New Britain and "Side By Side By Sondheim" at the Hidden Valley Country Club in Newington. The three reviews were published in the Newington Town Crier.

"Critic's Choice"—Paul Shipman and Ed Pizzella

My creative juices were flowing and I was bursting with impetuous desire to vary my theatrical experiences and exploit my penned-up creativity. The opportunity arrived with "The Prisoner Of Second Avenue." Matt and Mikki Zadrowski were doing the show in Middletown at the Oddfellows Hall and we assembled a group from TN to attend. It was done in proscenium and we thoroughly enjoyed it. In fact, we liked it so much that at the next TN meeting we voted to do it as our next production in Newington. Mikki suggested that we hire the fellow, who had just directed the Middletown show, Frank Camerata. We contacted him and he agreed to direct for us. In the meantime, we had so much success with our dinner-theatre productions that we decided to do "Prisoner" in the dinner-theatre format at the Indian Hill Country Club. Since there was no stage there, our plan was to do it in the round.

When we were about to schedule auditions, we invited Frank to an informal production meeting at our house. We frequently held meetings there, since Marge was TN's president. Frank had previously successfully directed for TN. He was an amiable, olive-skinned, short, thin man with black curly hair and thick glasses. He was beaming and enthusiastic, until we told him that we were going to do the show in the round. He suddenly displayed bewilderment and stuttered "You can't do this show in the round!"

He, of course, was referring to a number of essential technical effects which, at first blush, seemed to be impossible to perform without the proscenium's backstage maneuvering. The story takes place in a high-rise apartment building on Second Avenue in New York City and much of the action occurs on the balcony. The upstairs neighbor periodically screams down at the main characters and douses them with buckets of water. Snow comes down on the balcony and occasionally Mel, the main character, comes out to threaten the neighbor.

"You need a backstage to perform those tricks," Frank argued. He appeared to be quite distraught. I had been appointed the set and technical effects designer for the show. I calmed him down and assured him it could be done.

Frank Cammerata

The show was to be performed on an 18'x18' one-step platform in the middle of the banquet hall. On one side, I added a 3'x6' one-step platform, which would be the balcony. I built a 3'x6' wooden box about 24" high. This was to be placed on four columns elevated seven feet above the balcony platform. The top of the box was open and it was wired for electricity and sound. I installed a lamp, sound equipment and a snow machine. Holes and slits were provided to permit the snow (Styrofoam flakes) and water to be poured down. A trapdoor was installed to permit someone of diminutive stature to enter the box. Joe Neiman, a TN regular, offered his teenaged son as the technician. I'll never forget the expression on Frank's face, when we did a trial run. His previous negativity completely disappeared. He was ecstatic.

Although I had worked backstage on a number of productions, aside from my involvement with "Three On A Bench," this was my first of many ventures in set design and in the design and construction of set pieces and technical effects. Voila! Another creative genie had popped out of the bottle.

I auditioned for the leading role in "Prisoner," but I was no match for Bill Bianchi. How do you compete with a guy, who merely has to stand there to evoke uncontrollable laughter? I was cast as Harry, Mel's wealthy brother. I was disappointed, but I determined to make Harry outstanding. This is when I began to focus on character development. Every time I accepted a role thereafter, I would visualize the character and then change my appearance, my mannerisms, my movements and my vocal intonations and speech patterns to bring that character to life. I gave Harry a New York accent and a variety of distinctive Big Apple traits.

In one of the performances, I came up with the adlib that saved the day. Mel is a middle-aged corporate exec, who, after having faithfully served the company for many years, has been laid off and can't find another job. He becomes depressed and decides that his only salvation is to buy and run a summer camp in Vermont. He goes to his affluent brother, Harry, to borrow the $25,000.00 to buy the camp.

At first Harry is reluctant, believing that his brother has lost his marbles and that this idea is merely a whimsical flight of fancy. After giving the situation more thought, however, he goes to visit Mel to tell him that he has changed his mind and that he will finance the venture. As I hand him the check, saying "Here's the money! Now, go buy your summer camp," Mel sits on the sofa, which collapses, as one of its legs breaks unexpectedly. Without the slightest hesitation, I throw out the line "And while you're at it, buy yourself some new furniture." The adlib got the biggest laugh in the show.

The March 11, 1976 issue of the Newington Town Crier proclaimed that "Ed Pizzella, TN's 'Jack-of-all-parts and master of all' was superb as brother Harry. His even, deliberate, dry down-play of some excruciating lines was brilliant."

CHAPTER SIX

A TASTE OF WINTERGREEN

It was 1976 and the country was celebrating the Bicentennial of our nation's declaration of independence. All the social and civic organizations in town were asked to join the festivities by adopting some type of project that would appropriately memorialize that historic event. Theatre Newington decided to participate by doing the Gershwin political spoof, "Of Thee I Sing." I had recently suffered a political defeat and had some free time on my hands, so I was anxious to become involved.

The Ed Pizzella family ca. 1975. (L-R) Mike, Steve, Linda, Ed, Marge, Rick and Laura.

My brother Bob and I had worked for my law school classmate, Lew Rome, in his quest for the Republican gubernatorial nomination and in repayment I was appointed counsel for the Senate majority in the 1973 and 1974 legislative sessions. I also served as counsel for the Banks and Regulated Activities Committee. I gathered together a group of disaffected local Republicans and we succeeded in changing the leadership of the Town Committee. I strove to repair strained political relationships and by 1975 I was presented with the Republican nomination for mayor. By this time Democratic registrations far exceeded those of my party and, despite the valiant efforts of our base, my family and many friends, I again suffered a narrow loss to my Democratic friend, Joe Doyle.

Planting a campaign sign: Al Jorgensen and Ed Pizzella.

Steven, my eldest, celebrated his 18th birthday three weeks before the election and I was pleased to accompany him, when he registered to vote.

(L-R) Jean Taschner, Town Clerk, Steve and Ed Pizzella.

With five children traveling was prohibitive, so we rented a trailer and took up camping. The kids really enjoyed this pastime and I began to give some thought to buying a bus and converting it to a camper. I had a friend who worked at the town garage, Carlo Simone. He was a client and my barber's brother-in-law. I mentioned this idea to him and one afternoon in August he called me and said that the Town was auctioning off a school bus. I went to the auction and with a bid of $425.00 purchased a 1958 Dodge army bus that had been purchased as government surplus and used as a school bus. I had left my office in a rush and forgot to bring a check. Fortunately a friend of mine, Sheriff Bob Tracy, was present and loaned me the funds to consummate the deal. With the help of my TV repairman, Charlie Holmes, I converted it to a motor home and this was the symbol of my mayoral campaign.

Drawing by Charles Casalengo.

I was intrigued with the prospect of becoming involved with the first musical of my theatrical career and this is when I learned that you could perform the lead in a musical even if you weren't a "singer." I could become another Rex Harrison, my idol! Subconsciously, I think that I was also motivated by the idea that, if I couldn't win a political contest in the real world, I could at least obtain vicarious satisfaction by playing a victorious politician on stage.

I loved Gershwin and I had learned something about acting and politics. I now felt comfortable with my hairpiece and everything seemed to fall conveniently into place. I auditioned and was cast in the leading role of John P. Wintergreen, the bachelor presidential candidate who's swept into office on a tidal wave of love. During the campaign, he tours the country in search of his soul mate. In validation of the renowned motto, "amor omnia vincet," he finds her, wins the election and marries her. Richard Paulos of Meriden was chosen as musical director and Ralph Testa and Matt Zadrowski were the artistic co-directors.

I'll never forget the auditions. We held them in the Town Hall auditorium. The old high school had been converted to the Town Hall when the new high school was built on Willard Avenue. As TN's business manager, I had arranged an affiliation with the Parks and Recreation Department, which allowed us to use the Town Hall auditorium for auditions, rehearsals and performances without charge.

This show was truly a family affair. My eldest daughter, Laura, was then a teenager and I induced her to audition. She was cast in the role of one of beauty contest participants. Thank God she didn't win or there might have been an implication of incest. My wife, Marge, was the Stage Manager, my son, Rick, worked on set construction, and my eldest son, Steve, was an usher.

Laura Pizzella

Bill Bianchi—cast as Throttlebottom in "Of Thee I Sing."

This was a show with a large cast, but one of the hardest roles to fill was that of the Vice Presidential candidate, Throttlebottom. The character was all that the name implies. He is the consummate bumbler. We auditioned and auditioned, but there was no one who could do justice to the role. We were at our wits' end when finally Bill Bianchi walked in. The directors asked him to go up on stage and read from the script. As soon as he walked out on stage and before he could get a word out of his mouth, there were sprinkles of laughter among the horde of would-be cast and crew. As he paused, waiting for silence, the twitters grew into a tornado of rollicking laughter and applause. The auditions were over.

Now came the difficult task of putting the show together. There was so much to do. The first thing, of course, was to develop an overall concept for the production. I had read the book and there were a few things that bothered me. The show opens at a party celebrating Wintergreen's nomination on the 63rd ballot. The dialogue recounts the hilarious events of the topsy-turvy political convention leading to the nomination.

Well, I had been a devotee of national political conventions. As a teenager, I had spent many a summer afternoon listening to them as I was painting walls or hanging wallpaper. The only president I knew in my youth was FDR. I was twelve years old when he was running for his third term. I was glued to the radio during the Democratic and Republican national conventions. I enjoyed listening to the southern drawls, the western twangs and especially the colorful and interminable introductions that invariably preceded the announcement of each delegation's vote. "Mr. Chairman, the great state of Maine, the home of the lobster, the potato and the caribou . . . etc."

Whenever I thought of national politics, I could not get these vivid, exaggerated colloquial banterings out of my mind. "Why should we just talk about this fascinating, almost farcical interplay?" I said to the directors, "Let's do it! Instead of a victory party, let's open with the convention!" They liked the idea and we sat down to rewrite the opening.

One of the actors, who was playing the role of a southern senator, was Bill Wilbur, a scruffy, deep throated fellow whom I had met at the Hole In The Wall Theatre in New Britain. He was overpowering and had mastered the southern accent and mannerisms. With a huge wooden gavel, he chaired the convention. The audience was the convention floor.

Throughout the auditorium signs had been placed containing the names of the states. We wrote colorful dialogue and stationed members of the cast in strategic locations throughout the audience. The show opened with the bellowing Bill Wilbur gaveling the convention to order. Time and time again, he forcefully demanded that the aisles be cleared and the delegates seated. The convention was in the midst of the 63rd ballot. With a contingent of fellow actors, I waited breathlessly in the hallway at a side entrance to the chamber, unobserved by the audience.

When some semblance of order had been restored, the chair recognized the delegate from the "great State of Georgia, the home of the peanut, the peach and the boll weevil." The votes cast by this delegate dramatically threw the nomination to Wintergreen. The convention was immediately plunged into pandemonium. The band struck up "Swanee" and "The Battle Hymn Of The Republic" and I and my retinue dashed into the hall, running about shaking hands with, hugging and greeting confused patrons. This was one of the most exhilarating openings I had ever experienced in the more than a hundred productions in which I participated in my diverse theatrical career.

TN Regulars (L-R), Marge Clauson, Ed Pizzella,
Shyrlee Burr and Charlotte Downard Testa.

We did some other interesting things in this show. This was a multimedia event. The last scene before intermission was the recap of the national campaign. The book required stills to be projected on a screen, depicting various campaign stops nationwide. We decided, instead, to shoot and display some videos. I recalled that there was a railroad car in front of the Yankee Silversmith Restaurant on Route 5 in Wallingford. We contacted the restaurant and obtained their permission to shoot a video there. We gathered the cast and a group of extras and headed for Wallingford. My supporters collected at the rear of the railcar and cheered, as I stood on the rear platform pontificating and kissing babies, while the cameras rolled.

But the funniest footage was shot right there at the Newington Town Hall. A platform was placed next to the entrance to the Police Department and there I stood, delivering an eloquent address before a throng of enthusiastic supporters. On the periphery of the crowd was a little girl, listening and intently sucking on a big red lollipop. Stalking her was Throttlebottom, the vice-presidential candidate. Suddenly, he grabs the candy from the screaming child and runs off. After a chase through the mob, we see him apprehended by two of Newington's finest. The next scene takes place in the police department's lock-up, as Throttlebottom frantically grasps the bars that restrain him and begs for his freedom.

One of the lessons I learned in this production is that actors can sometimes be quite dispensable. I also witnessed the application of the familiar axiom, "The show must go on." A close friend, Bill Pollack had been cast in the meaty supporting role of a prominent and extremely verbose southern senator. It was our final performance and the cast was in the dressing room being made up and getting into costume. It was 7:30 pm and we were going up at 8:00 o'clock. Senator Claghorn, as I kiddingly called him,—I can't remember the character's name—was nowhere to be found. Suddenly the telephone rang. It was Jean Pollack, Bill's wife, informing us that he was seriously ill and confined to bed. We refused to panic. The directors called the cast together in a huddle. We hurriedly perused the script and reassigned Bill's lines. When the curtain came down, no one in the audience even noticed the absence of the blustering Senator Claghorn.

CHAPTER SEVEN

DOWN FOR THE COUNT

Theatre Newington's "Count Dracula"—(L-R) Prof.
VanHelsing, Renfield, Dr. Seward and the attendant.

I had now appeared in thirteen shows and had added gravitas to my blossoming theatrical resume, but I still hadn't done anything of a dramatic, or perhaps melodramatic, nature. And now Theatre Newington was doing "Count

Dracula," the Ted Tiller version. This was the stage version of the Bram Stoker novel most familiar to American audiences. Needless to say, having been relegated to a mere supporting role in "Prisoner," my last non-musical stage venture, I was itching for a lead. I attended the auditions and gave it my all. I was devastated when I was denied the role of Dracula and offered that of Professor Van Helsing. Although the disappointment was crushing, I was determined to make, what I thought was a "subordinate" character, spectacular.

It wasn't until I read the novel and reread the script that I realized that Dracula was the titular lead, but that the actual lead was Professor Van Helsing.

"Count Dracula"—Charlotte Downard Testa as Mina, and
Ed Pizzella, as Professor Heinrich Van Helsing.

Here's where my linguistic abilities would prove invaluable. I didn't really know much about the Dutch language, so I combined hints of French and German accents to create my own concept of a Dutch accent. By this time in my theatrical career, I had developed the knack of drastically changing my physical appearance with each role. I went to the Salvation Army store and purchased an oversized, blue pinstriped, double-breasted suit. This I stuffed with a pillow to create a plausible paunch. Offstage I was accustomed to wearing a hairpiece and I was not normally adorned with facial hair. I discarded the rug, grayed and disheveled my hair, added a moustache, a goatee, wire-rimmed spectacles, a meerschaum pipe and some flamboyant gestures and Voila!—Professor Heinrich Van Helsing, the eccentric and bombastic Dutch vampire expert in the flesh.

I again had the pleasure of working with Bill Bianchi, who was cast as Dr. Seward, Mina's guardian. Bill had a great deal of stage presence and he was very expressive and easy to work with, but he had one glaring fault, which I now learned to my dismay. He was plagued by an unreliable memory and would frequently lose his line. I didn't realize this when we did "Of Thee I Sing," because in that show we didn't have many scenes together where just the two of us had dialogue. In "Count Dracula," I learned how much an actor is compelled to rely on his fellow actors.

I liked Bill very much and I didn't want to appear condescending or to belittle or offend him, so I took it upon myself to memorize his lines, as well as my own, and, whenever he might have a lapse, I would simply feed him his line. This proved to be so effective that in many instances the audience thought that it was I who had faltered.

I was dazzled by the show's special effects and, in particular, the manner in which we were able to make Dracula vanish into thin air. Vampires, of course, are terrified by sunlight, which instantly deprives them of their evil powers. One of Van Helsing's ploys was to engage Dracula in conversation and distract him until dawn and, when the first rays of sunlight made him vulnerable, to seize him. When

Dracula realizes that the sun has risen, he avoids the trap by simply vanishing.

To accomplish this, we constructed a hidden door in the lower portion of the upstage wall. When the sun comes up, Dracula abruptly dons his hood (which is attached to the neck of his cape) and, with his back to the audience, heads upstage (toward the trap door) searching for a means of escape. Dr. Seward and I are on each side of him and we grab his shoulders to restrain him. Using wire hangers, we had constructed a collapsible framework that was sewn into the hood and shoulders of his cape. When the three of us arrive at the hidden panel door, Seward and I pretend to struggle with him, pulling the cape from side to side. Dracula, in the meantime, with the help of a couple of stagehands and obscured from sight by the flowing cape, drops down on his knees and escapes through the hidden door. Despite the fact that Dracula has left the stage, it appears to the audience that he's still there because of the wire structure inside the cape and our feigned struggle to restrain him.

Dracula having left the stage and the trap door having been closed, we drop the empty cape (containing the now collapsed wire framework) and the audience is amazed to find that the vampire has virtually disappeared before their very eyes.

The show was moderately successful, although some theatre aficionados disagreed with the portrayal of Dracula as an exaggerated, over made-up, superficial, comedic caricature, rather than a subtle, sinister, sexually attractive, romantic figure. When all was said and done, the November 4, 1976 issue of the Town Crier reported that "Ed Pizzella was the stick out performer in the experienced cast. The Theatre Newington veteran gave a vigorous portrayal of Professor Heinrich Van Helsing, a specialist called in to cure the ward of an old friend. Pizzella maintained a difficult accent throughout the proceedings and was generally relaxed, yet confident in his performance."

Since the Mark Twain Masquers were scheduled to do this show three months hence at the Roberts Theatre in West Hartford, they sent several of their officers to see our rendition. The next morning, I received a telephone call from their treasurer, who asked if I'd be willing to play the role of Van Helsing in their upcoming production. This group had an outstanding, almost professional, reputation and I had dreamed of working with them. I was extremely flattered and awed by the offer and accepted without hesitation.

The Roberts Theatre is located on the campus of the Kingswood-Oxford School on Troutbrook Road in West Hartford. When I appeared at the read-through I was thoroughly mesmerized. Except as an usher at the State Theatre in Hartford during my high school days, I had never worked in a real theatre. I introduced myself to the rest of the cast and a guide was assigned to show us around this marvelous facility.

The backstage dressing rooms were spacious and luxurious. An unbelievable variety of costumes were stored in the basement. The lighting and sound systems were state-of-the-art. In the backstage wall there was a huge double door, which must have measured eight feet wide and sixteen feet high. This led to a massive scene shop, which contained every imaginable power tool and every conceivable type of building material. There was even a well with a motorized hoist on which an eighteen or twenty foot canvas drop could be hung. This permitted the artist to stand at floor level and, without moving a muscle, paint any portion of the canvas by simply operating the hoist.

Large segments of a set would be constructed in the scene shop and then rolled on casters through the massive backstage door onto the stage. But the contrivance that thrilled me the most was the hydraulic apron, which ran the whole width of the stage and projected out into the audience. It could be silently lowered to a variety of positions and even to a depth of fifteen feet below stage level, where it could be accessed by means of an elevator located backstage. With the apron lowered, it could be set and actors positioned without these preparations being visible to the audience.

The director was a petit woman who had been hired as regular employee to direct all their shows. She was assertive and extremely knowledgeable in theatre matters.

I was amazed by how a show could be uniquely shaped by a director's individual interpretation of the script. Dracula in this show was played by Bob Donnelly, who had appeared as Mel Edison in the Masquers' production of "The Prisoner Of Second Avenue." He was a subtle and subdued, yet sinister, sexually attractive and exotic, romantic figure. I was also astonished when the director made numerous cuts in the dialogue, which manifested and developed her unique interpretation.

I developed a friendship with John Dignan, who played the role of Dr. Seward. He was a tall, thin, gray haired man, who spoke in an erudite and affected manner with a hint of a British accent. John had poor eyesight and, whenever there was a blackout or we were near the edge of the stage, he would lean on me for support.

Dean Keithline, an extremely attractive young lady, played Mina. I enjoyed saving her from the clutches of Dracula and I'll never forget the incredibly artistic photo that was taken of the two of us by Roger Dollarhyde, a professional photographer, and used to publicize the show. In it I am holding up a crucifix and Mina, having assumed some of the characteristics of a vampire, recoils in fright.

The rehearsals went well and we finally progressed to hell week, the week before opening night. The director asked us to come to tech rehearsal, the Sunday before opening night, in full make-up and costume. My wife, Marge, and Flo Becker, a neighbor and hairdresser, helped me with my make-up and I took on the elderly, paunchy and somewhat comedic appearance I had used in the Newington show. I removed the rug, grayed, disheveled and sprayed my hair, pasted on a moustache and goatee, put on my wire-rimmed spectacles, donned my oversized, double-breasted, pinstriped suit, stuffed with a pillow, and, when I presented myself on the set with my meerschaum pipe stuck in my mouth, I was immediately confronted by the director, who appeared quite perturbed and, with the threatening air of a communist border guard, ordered me to leave, "since outsiders were not permitted on the set during rehearsals." She was quite embarrassed when she learned it was I, but she was pleased with the metamorphosis.

In contrast with the Newington show, this production played to packed audiences and was received with great enthusiasm. The show was well paced and the technical effects were stupendous. In playing this role, I experienced moments of extreme exhilaration, which I encountered nowhere else in my lengthy theatrical career.

The play is performed in three acts and the last act has two scenes. Van Helsing's goal is to save Mina by killing Dracula. During the play the Professor has enlightened us about the pernicious proclivities of the vampire and his vulnerabilities. We learn that he is a nocturnal creature, that it is at night when his nefarious powers are most dangerous, that sunlight makes him impotent and that he is most vulnerable when he's sleeping in his coffin during the daylight hours. The Professor's plan is to find Dracula's crypt and at the crack of dawn, while he is asleep and powerless, to drive a wooden stake through his heart.

The first two acts and the first scene of the third act take place in Dr. Seward's asylum. These portions of the play are thus performed on the stage with the apron lowered to a point below the audience's sightline. In the meantime, the apron has been set with Dracula's elevated coffin surrounded by gray and dismal boulders and debris covered with eons of dust and eerie cobwebs. The coffin is equipped with a canister filled with sand which, at the end of the show, will be placed at the vampire's armpit and into which the stake is to be ceremoniously driven.

During the first scene of the third act, Dracula and Mina have descended backstage and, unseen by the audience, have taken their positions on the lowered apron, Dracula lying in the coffin and Mina behind a boulder, ready to protect him from harm. The first scene ends with Van Helsing, appropriately armed with stake and mallet and pursued by Dr. Seward, racing out of the asylum and headed for the crypt at Castle Carfax.

During the blackout which follows (no curtain is used), the apron slowly and mysteriously rises, accompanied by the discordant, ear piercing sounds of suspenseful music and the spooky atmosphere created by an abundance of billowing fog and illuminated by a scintillating strobe and sinister green spotlight. The unexpected and morbid appearance of the rising crypt elicits shrieks and applause. The set, which had been used in the prior two and a half acts, is left dark and, when the apron reaches stage level, the lights come up low, as Dr. Seward and I enter the crypt and rush toward the coffin.

Mina, who is now fully under the vampire's influence, attempts to shield the coffin containing the sleeping Count and is forcibly removed by Dr. Seward. Then having carefully positioned the stake on the Count's chest (actually in the canister of sand), with three well aimed strokes of the large wooden mallet, I dramatically drive the stake into the vampire's evil heart. The sound of each of the strokes is immensely amplified and accompanied by reverberation and blood curdling screams, as the vampire's blood spurts in all directions and Dracula wildly flails his arms and legs. The stimulating combination of spectacular lighting, sound and applause was so exhilarating that I feared I'd collapse.

A review in the February 1, 1977 issue of the Hartford Courant noted that "Edward Pizzella imbues the Dutch vampire specialist, Dr. Van Helsing, with solid Teutonic optimism," while the February 3rd issue of the Town Crier carried the headline, "PIZZELLA REPEATS FINE PERFORMANCE IN DRACULA." The article went on to say that "The man who stole the show in the Newington production recreates the role of Professor Heinrich Van Helsing for the Masquers. He is Newington's own Ed Pizzella and his performance has prospered in the transition . . . . As Van Helsing, Ed Pizzella is energetic and thoroughly engaging. He brings both humor and humanity to his role." The Connecticut Jewish Ledger on the same date opined that "As a visiting vampire specialist, Edward G. Pizzella is properly foreign-sounding and profound."

Sometime later, I learned through the grapevine that the Masquers were accustomed to present annual awards for outstanding performances and that I had been nominated for my role in this show, but was not qualified to receive the award because I was not a member of that group.

Another eleven years would pass before I would be granted a third opportunity to whack the Count. About ten years after the Masquers' production, I joined with a group of thespians to form Theatre One Productions, Inc. We had entered into an agreement with L'Auberge D'Elegance, a banquet facility on Route 6 in Bristol, to produce dinner theatre. "Count Dracula" was our eighth show.

This production was vastly different from the prior two versions. This one was presented in three-quarters. It was directed by Fred Miller, who was known in theatrical circles as Lance Samia. Lance was an engineer who had worked as a male stripper. He was a marvel with special effects and a very intuitive director.

Four years earlier he had directed "Bell, Book And Candle" for the Hole In The Wall Theatre. He had induced me to audition for his show, although I was reluctant to do so because I had recently auditioned for "Guys & Dolls" with the Onstage Performers, who were then doing dinner theatre at the Embassy Room in Wolcott. I was up front with him and when I was offered the leading role in both shows, I chose to do Nathan Detroit in the musical. My decision to do the Wolcott show must have been a boon to Barbara Gallow, a very talented actress who had been chosen for the female lead in Lance's show, because the stage manager replaced me as the male lead and she subsequently married him.

At L'Auberge, the show was done in the three-quarters format. I enjoyed this theatrical mode, because it offers the actor an opportunity for intimate contact with the audience. I vividly remember the scene when I would lecture Jonathan and Dr. Seward about the proclivities of vampires. The lines are excruciating and build to a climax, after which I make an abrupt and dramatic exit. Although this was not the end of the scene, in virtually every performance my departure elicited applause and it took me several minutes backstage to wind down from my fever pitch.

Bob Dio, a local radio personality, did an exceptional job as Dracula, who closely resembled the West Hartford rendition of the titular lead. I worked with Lance on the special effects and learned a great deal about scrims and flash pots. In the end, I had succeeded in playing the very same flamboyant, quirky, but comedic and lovable hero in three very different theatrical environments. Apparently, I had grown in the progression and my efforts prompted the Waterbury Republican in its October 7, 1988 issue to comment that, "Ed Pizzella, as Professor Heinrich Van Helsing, delivers the most passionate performance of the play."

Between my two melodramatic exploits, TN was doing "Barefoot In The Park," as a dinner-theatre production at Indian Hill Country Club. Edith Zeldes was directing and Bill Bianchi was cast as Velasco. He played the role as a comedic, slapstick character, without an accent and without the depth which I felt was essential to make him third-dimensional.

I did the set design and George Burr and I built the set. Dave Fitzgerald did the lighting and my son Rick handled sound.

I induced the director to allow me to insert and direct a short comic scene between the first two acts. Act I takes place in the empty fifth floor apartment with the young married couple anxiously awaiting the delivery of their furniture. The script mentions the moving company, the Santini Brothers, and alludes to the difficulty of delivering heavy furniture up five flights of stairs. I suggested that TN order T-shirts with the inscription "The Santini Bros. Moving & Storage Co." At the end of the first act, I had the stage crew, wearing the T-shirts and doused with buckets of water, laboriously and clumsily carting the furniture onto the set with Velasco gesturing in mime and directing the placement of the various set pieces. The scene got a big laugh.

But the joke was on me because, years later, on one of my many trips to New York City to spend the day and see a Broadway show, I was stunned to see a large box truck with the eye-catching sign, "Santini Bros. Moving & Storage." It was then that I first realized that Neil Simon in his many creative works was nevertheless compelled to rely on reality and frequently referred to real people and real names.

CHAPTER EIGHT

IMMERSED IN THE HOLE

It was 1977 and, although I now had fifteen shows under my belt, I was driven to learn more about intimate theatre. Several years before, I had attended the Hole In The Wall's production of "Casablanca" at the little bookstore on Allen Street in New Britain. The show was adapted for the stage and directed by Ray Shinn. The action literally took place in the midst of the audience and clever technical effects were employed to compensate for the absence of a set.

An example of this was the climactic ending of the show, when the plane takes off at the airport. Speakers were attached to the ceiling in sequence from one side of the room to the other, so that, with the motor sounds passing overhead across the room from one speaker to the next, the audience can actually visualize the plane taking off. Years later I used this very same technique, when I produced and directed this show at the L'Auberge d'Elegance Dinner Theatre on Route 6 in Bristol.

The Hole was a place seething with theatrical experimentation. This was a learning place. No two shows were ever produced in the same manner. Most theatre groups adopt a form they feel comfortable with and stick to it show after show. It might be proscenium, the round or three-quarters. Whatever it might be, they'd stick with it. And likewise with their brand of theatre. Most theatre groups adhere to conventional shows, those that are tried and true.

Not so with the Hole, every show was different in every respect and the avant-garde was preferred.

Even the people were different. Most community theatre groups are composed of middle-aged, middle class folks seeking light-hearted diversion. At the Hole, most of the participants are either college professors or students, who are young, poor and obsessed. While most theatre groups have strict membership rules and a recognized organizational structure, at the Hole, anyone who comes in off the street is a member, there's no board of directors and there are no officers. A chairman is elected to preside at each meeting and show proposals are presented and voted upon. The proposal is presented by the would-be producer and each show has its own separate and distinct organization, which includes director, stage manager, set designer, etc.

This was a place where theatrical impulses were free to run wild and I enjoyed learning. I was particularly attracted to their unique brand of intimate theatre. Here an actor could have direct contact with the audience and I loved it.

I had gotten to know Ray Shinn and he invited me to audition for "An Ideal Husband," an Oscar Wilde piece he was directing for the Hole In The Wall. HITW was then located in the basement of the Congregational Church located on the southwest corner of Arch and Main Streets in New Britain. I was cast in the supporting role of Lord Caversham and was anxious to experience HITW's unique brand of theatre.

Like "Casablanca," the show was performed in the midst of the audience. After one of my entrances, I removed my overcoat and handed it to an attractive young lady in the audience to hold while I was performing. When I was making my exit, I went over to her, gave her a smile, took back my coat and left.

Cast of "R.U.R." Ed Pizzella, as Jacob Berman, seated. Standing (L-R), John Powers, Ted Guhl and Mark Farnloff.

In the next show, "R.U.R.," I was cast in the dramatic role of Jacob Berman, the treasurer of a company that has produced robots so self-sufficient that they decided to take over the world and relegate human beings to the status of slaves. My big scene came at the end of the play when Berman, seeing that the robots are about to attack the plant, goes berserk and dashes out to his death. The July 14, 1977 issue of the Town Crier remarked that "Pizzella did an equally fine job as an old, whacked-out, stereotype professor." Then came "Time Of Your Life."

This show presented me with some amazing revelations, which greatly assisted me in my quest to learn more about intimate theatre. This Saroyan piece takes place in a seedy bar on the docks of San Francisco. Dave Curran and Ted Guhl, both well respected and veteran actors, had leading roles and Ray Shinn directed. I was cast in the supporting role of the Society Gentleman. The entire church basement was the set with the bar located on the wall opposite the theatre entrance, booths on the side walls and tables in the center. The walls and ceiling were draped with nets, buoys and a variety of nautical paraphernalia. A number of seats in the midst of the audience were reserved for cast members. Among the characters in the play there was a police officer and McCarthy, the Irish longshoreman.

The entrance to the theatre was at the rear of the building in a lovely courtyard, where the audience gathered before the show and during intermissions. Before the doors opened, the cast, made-up and in costume, one by one, drifted out into the courtyard to mingle in character with the audience. The actor, who played the role of the policeman, made an authentic entrance, when he was dropped off by a police cruiser and entered the courtyard from the street. When the doors opened, the actors entered the theatre with the audience. The bar too was authentic and beer was served to the audience during the show. The audience was enthralled as the actors in their midst assumed their respective roles.

Ray Shinn was a marvelous director, but he was definitely a light weight, when it came to the use of accents or dialects to assist in character development. The actor who played the role of McCarthy did an acceptable job, but I thought he could have done a great deal more to make the character outstanding by employing physical enhancements and through the use of an accent.

Most of our shows were on Friday and Saturday nights, but during this run there was a Saturday matinee. The cast got together on the Wednesday night before the matinee for a pick-up rehearsal. This is when we learned that the actor playing McCarthy would not be able to do the matinee. The director desperately searched for a replacement. When no volunteers came forth, he approached me. I told him I'd do it, if he'd let me play McCarthy my way. He agreed.

I had played the Society Gentleman in a very sophisticated manner. I wore a hairpiece and a white dinner jacket. For McCarthy, I removed the rug, padded my waist and wore a pea coat and longshoreman's cap. My son, Steve, is a plumber. He loaned me a pair of old work boots that were completely worn out and headed for the trash bin. The same Irish brogue that distinguished John Fitzgerald in "Suds

In Your Eye" and Officer Callahan in "Three On A Bench" completed the seedy longshoreman. No announcement was made and there was no opportunity to change the program. After the matinee, not a soul in attendance had the slightest inkling that the Society Gentleman and McCarthy were played by the same actor.

Ed Pizzella and Karen Gronbeck

Beside the thrill of intimate contact with the audience, I was attracted to this brand of theatre by the fact that each show ran for six weekends. Every show I had previously participated in ran one or two weekends, at the most. After rehearsing for six or eight weeks and investing so much time, effort and energy in developing a unique stage character, it was always a let-down to display the fruits of my labor in only two or four performances. After all, a non-equity actor's only remuneration is the gratification he derives from the audience's appreciation of his work. That appreciation is expressed in terms of laughter, tears or applause, and an actor never gets enough.

CHAPTER NINE

A TOUCH OF THE DRAMATIC

It was a balmy Sunday afternoon in the summer of 1977. I was sitting in a lounge chair on the lush green grass of my sister's backyard, comfortably wrapped in the radiant glow of the midday sun. In my lap Arthur Miller's brilliant script, "A View From The Bridge," was being drenched by a stream of tears cascading down my cheeks. The warm bucolic silence was periodically broken by the muffled, sporadic sobs that would occasionally make good their escape from my otherwise relaxed, semiconscious body.

Louise Chiaputti, Ed Pizzella's sister.

Suddenly, I was jerked back to consciousness by the touch of a hand on my shoulder, as a whisper behind me plaintively inquired, "What's wrong? Is there anything I can do?" It was the concerned voice of my sister, Weeze (an endearing corruption of Louise). As familiar as I was with that voice, I didn't immediately recognize it. I guess that was because she normally spoke in a high decibel range, breathlessly barking orders, edicts, criticisms, altercations and invectives in an endless tirade. But now her voice was soft as velvet. She was worried.

I had just gone through a heart-rending marital separation. After twenty-one years of marriage, punctuated by valiant efforts to reverse the inevitable, Marge and I finally reached the point of no return. Our ill-fated union had produced five wonderful children, whom we both loved very much. In order to minimize the disruptive impact of our separation, it was I who left with literally no more than the shirt on my back. Love had long ago abandoned our relationship and the trauma of a physical separation was something I had reluctantly anticipated and emotionally wrestled with for a long time. I dreaded leaving because I desperately feared that I would become estranged from my children and family, to me, was the most important thing in life. I was resigned to the fact that there was no other course and, on a Sunday morning after we returned from church, I tearfully broke the news.

I was still on an emotional roller coaster after my marital breakup and, when the Hole In The Wall Theatre of New Britain announced auditions for "A View From The Bridge," I scampered to obtain a copy of Arthur Miller's moving script and, as I read it, I could feel the pathos in my bones. I was a lawyer and the son of Italian immigrants. The connection was irresistible. I could feel the lure of my heritage. I was determined to go to the auditions that night and claim my rightful role of the lawyer, Alfieri, for I was the bridge in real life.

Dave Curran

Dave Curran, a veteran actor whom I greatly admired, was directing. I was surprised when Ray Shinn came to audition. Try as I might, the best I could do was to be offered the supporting role of Marco, the elder brother wetback and Ray Shinn would play the coveted role of Alfieri. Arlene Mann of Manchester was cast in the role of Beatrice and the role of Eddie Carbone would be played by Peter LoFreddo of Middletown. I was crushed. What was Curran doing? Was this just another example of HITW politics?

Arlene Mann as Beatrice   Peter Lofreddo as Eddie Carbone

Dave Curran was incredibly perceptive. I was amazed at his grasp of the nuts and bolts of my Italian heritage, his understanding of old world principles and immigrant attitudes and his ability to convincingly portray the distinctly ethnic nuances so essential to the effective creation of empathy. I was also impressed by the group's all-encompassing creativity, the constantly probing innovative spirit and the overwhelming totality of effort that was devoted by numerous volunteers to make this production an unqualified success.

Again, the entire theatre became the set. The action takes place in Red Hook, New York, near the Brooklyn Bridge. One member of the crew was a photography buff, so we gathered the cast together on a Sunday and drove to New York City, where we visited all of the areas mentioned in the script and took pictures of the Brooklyn Bridge, the front stoops and the storefronts in Little Italy. We returned with more than three hundred photos.

"A View From The Bridge"—Ray Shinn as Alfieri and Ed Pizzella as Marco.

Platforms were built and seats for the audience were placed in the center of the theatre. Another member of the crew was an artist. A ramp was built along the back wall and, using the photos, the artist painted a mural of the Brooklyn Bridge that extended along the entire length of the rear wall. The mural must have been forty feet long and special lighting was used to create a third dimensional image. The phone booth was placed on one of the sidewalls and the interior of the apartment was located on a platform against the front wall. Again using the photos, front stoops and storefronts were painted in perspective on the sidewalls. The floor was painted to look like cobblestones and included was a manhole where the death scene was to take place. When you entered the theatre, you would swear you were on a street in Red Hook.

I still tingle when I recall our intense rehearsals and the realistic effects we developed to make the action believable. We diligently worked on a blood bag for Eddie Carbone. After a great deal of experimentation, we came up with a contrivance so realistic it was eerie. At one point in the show, when I display my anger and hint at the violent death scene that is to follow, I have to lift a dining room chair shoulder high gripping only the bottom of one leg. I practiced tirelessly until I perfected this maneuver.

We rehearsed the fight scene using a butter knife. I shivered at dress rehearsal when we finally used a real switchblade. I used an authentic Italian accent and, with the director's consent, added bits of Italian dialogue for realism. In one performance, when the fight ended and Eddie had been stabbed with his own knife, the gush of blood was so realistic that a couple of young ladies in the front row screamed with fright and jumped from their seats.

"A View From The Bridge"—Marco lifts the chair in anger.

My father had an old friend, who spoke with a thick Italian accent and played the mandolin, Tony Garofalo. I contacted him and he agreed to sit in the audience during each performance and play Italian music during the scene changes. My mother baked Italian cookies, which were sold from a pushcart during intermissions. Is it any wonder that this production earned me the most flattering reviews I ever received in my entire theatrical career.

"A View From The Bridge"—The Carbones at dinner

The October 27, 1977 issue of the Town Crier commented that "Ed Pizzella's Marco is true Italian all the way and his transition from quiet manner to raging anger is ably portrayed," while the October 28,1977 issue of The New Britain Herald remarked that "Ed Pizzella is the character most likely to be remembered. This is the gentlemanly, tough, determined immigrant. He will work hard, save, one day go back to claim his wife and children. Pizzella gives the part a sense of dignity and purpose. His accent is right; his gentleness and old world courtliness—this in a big, strong, working man, rings true."

And the November 2, 1977 issue of the New Haven Advocate concluded that "Ed Pizzella's portrayal of Marco (one of two illegal aliens whom Eddie and Beatrice hide in their home) lent an undeniable authenticity to the production. The son of Italian immigrant parents, Pizzella brought his own knowledge of Italian language and inflection into the play in a manner that Miller himself should not have omitted."

"A View From The Bridge" at Little Theatre of Manchester. Ed Garfield as Alfieri with Charlie Holmes directly behind.

Four years later, Little Theatre of Manchester decided to do this show and someone from that group contacted Arlene Mann, who had played the female lead in the New Britain production. She attempted to contact our original cast and those of us who were available were invited to audition. The Manchester group, at this point, were producing their shows at East Catholic High School in Manchester. We auditioned and Arlene was cast as Beatrice, I was cast as Marco, Tony Valenches was given the role of Eddie Carbone, Ed Garfield would play Alfieri and Barbara Gallow would play Eddie's niece. Directing was Bob Donnelly, who had played Count Dracula in the Mark Twain Masquers' production.

Charlie Holmes of Vernon was my TV repairman. I had known him for many years and he had become a personal friend. Charlie had helped me convert an old school bus, which I had purchased at auction from the Town of Newington, to a motor home. We were having difficulty filling out the cast and I induced Charlie to audition. Although he had never been on stage, Charlie was cast as one of the longshoremen. The show was successful, but it did not rise to the prominence of the earlier New Britain production.

The March 4, 1982 issue of The Manchester Herald remarked that "Responding to clear acting challenges, the cast is uniformly capable, with special kudos to Ed Pizzella who plays Marco, Tony Valenches who plays the difficult role of soul sick Eddie and Arlene Mann who plays the part of the long suffering wife," and The Glastonbury Citizen's issue of that date commented that "Pizzella's characterization of the bulwark between Eddie and his rival is quiet, solid, determined and convincing."

CHAPTER TEN

TRIUMPHS AND TRIBULATION

"Dark Of The Moon"—Ed Pizzella, as Preacher Haggler, and Paul Tosto.

It was 1978 and I was doing the rounds from one theatre group to another, looking for challenging roles. TN was doing "Dark Of The Moon" at Indian Hill Country Club. Charlotte Testa was directing and I nailed down the coveted role of the fire and brimstone evangelist, Preacher Haggler. I can still feel the exhilarating high that captivated me every time I catapulted out on the stage to deliver my impassioned sermon. It was in this show that I learned how important an adlib could be in an informative sense, rather than merely as a cover.

At dress rehearsal, one of the actors missed his cue and failed to make his entrance in a scene in which his dialogue was essential to provide necessary information to advance the plot. I was waiting for my entrance cue and realized that there was no way he could now gracefully get out on stage. After I made my entrance, I adlibbed the missing information so effectively that the director never noticed the miscue.

"Dark Of The Moon" was a success and then followed three outstanding productions at the Hole In The Wall in New Britain. "South Pacific" was always one of my favorite musicals. When I found out that the New Britain group had decided to do this show, I rushed to the library and obtained a copy of the book, "Tales Of The South Pacific." I sucked up as much background as I could, so that I could acquire a feel for the setting of this moving story and I prepared myself for the auditions. I learned that reading around a script is an essential exercise in such preparation.

Ted Guhl was directing and Ray Shinn provided the piano accompaniment. The hectic auditions were held in the basement of the church on the corner of Arch and Main. The cast was extremely large, so the auditions were crowded and grueling. After we finished, all of the hopeful contenders met at the Brown Derby on Allen Street to hear the casting announcements. I wanted the role of Emile deBecque so desperately, I could taste it.

During the auditions, I had met and became friendly with Virginia Vilcinskas of Berlin. She was a teacher in East Hampton and had just acquired a Doberman puppy named Ajax and was having a difficult time house training him. She would often appear at the theatre bleary-eyed and exhausted from cleaning up after the lovable, but incontinent canine. She had auditioned for the female lead and we sat together in a booth at the Brown Derby filled with anxiety, breathlessly waiting for the vital pronouncements that would determine the course of our lives for the next three months. Finally the word came down. Debra Caswell of Berlin was cast as the female lead and I was cast in the role of deBecque. I attempted to console Ginny, who was cast as one of the nurses.

We started our rehearsals in the church basement, but the show opened in September in the new theatre on Smalley Street. The building had been a plumbing supply warehouse, until HITW moved in and made the necessary renovations. The producers decided to make this production special. Truckloads of sand were purchased and three to four inches of the granular substance was spread on all of the floors throughout the theatre. Many of the musical numbers were choreographed and you can imagine how difficult it was to move gracefully in this totally unstable environment.

This production provided me with the unique opportunity to take full advantage of my linguistic skills. I recalled my experiences in French class at Weaver High and as President of the French Club. I recalled the emphasis my French teacher, Miss Phillips, had placed on pronunciation. With the director's approval, I used a French accent during rehearsals. I started with a fairly heavy inflection and then, as time went on, consulting with the director, I gradually lightened it until there was only a hint of an accent. I learned that a real accent never works on stage, because, no matter how clearly you try to enunciate, there will still be some members of the audience who will find it either distracting or difficult to understand some portions of the dialogue. On stage we strive for realism, not reality.

I derived immense pleasure singing directly to the audience in this intimate setting and I got the biggest kick out of working with the kids, who played my children. I can still feel the warm glow I felt when I made my entrance at the end of the show and sang "Dites Moi" to the children. The most flattering compliments I received were from members of the audience, who came to me and said that they thought my French accent was real and were absolutely convinced that Debbie and I were really in love.

I was pleased when the September 22, 1978 issue of The Herald reported that "Ed Pizzella is believable as deBecque, particularly as the smitten lover of 'Some Enchanted Evening'" and when the October 5, 1978 issue of the Newington Town Crier commented that "Ed Pizzella and Debra Caswell both have strong and wonderful voices and their songs together and separately were very well done. Ed seemed most at home when he had the opportunity to sing directly to his audience, while Debra seemed to prefer a more formal presentation." But even more complimentary was the statement in the October 20, 1978 issue of the Inferno, the Central Connecticut State College newspaper (it had not yet become a university), that "Ed Pizzella's portrayal of Emile deBecque was convincing, very convincing."

One of the things that endeared me to this show was the fact that I was familiar with most of the music and had derived so much pleasure from listening to the resonant and mellifluous voice of the famous Ezio Pinza on the original cast album. When the show closed, the cast presented me with a t-shirt which contained the inscription, "Edzio Pinzella."

My divorce had become final and Ginny and I were dating. I had started a new chapter in my life and years later, when someone we encountered would ask where we met, I would laughingly respond, "in the South Pacific."

My triumph in this musical was followed by the most humiliating experience of my extensive theatrical career. HITW had decided that their second show in the new theatre would be Shakespeare's "Romeo And Juliet" directed by the idiosyncratic Ray Shinn. Ray decided to update the Bard. He would set this famous and familiar piece in a discotheque. I allowed myself to be cast in the role of Lord Montague and night after night we were compelled to endure the deplorable humiliation of watching confused and irate members of the audience rise en masse in the midst of the performance, indignantly turn their backs to us and abruptly leave the theatre in a huff. This alarming image left an indelible scar on my theatrical psyche, marring what was otherwise a pleasant collection of nostalgic memories.

The abominable humiliation of "Romeo And Juliet" was sympathetically soothed by the subsequent exhilaration of "Man Of LaMancha." I had seen this show a number of years earlier and concluded that it was unquestionably the best musical play ever written. The storyline was a spiritually lifting and irresistibly moving depiction of the teachings of the Bible, the Ten Commandments and the Golden Rule, all rolled into one and liberally sprinkled with bits of Pygmalion. The music was poignant and melodic and the movement captivating. From that moment on, I longed to play the role of the whimsical Don Quixote.

The show was directed by Justine Tobis, a paralegal with a Hartford law firm, who subsequently passed the bar and who coincidentally was Dave Curran's girlfriend. Dave was the show's producer and, of course, was cast in the leading role, which suggested to me that the whole thing was a setup. Dave didn't have a great voice, but he was truly a great actor. It was from him that I learned that acting ability tops musical skill every time, i. e. a good actor can make you believe he's a good or at least an adequate singer. And Dave was a convincing actor.

Justine Tobis

Before I auditioned for the show, I did my traditional background research. I obtained a copy of Cervantes' work and read as much as I could about the principal character and the era in which the story takes place. I was so impressed with Don Quixote and the manner in which his story is presented that I subsequently wrote a poem entitled, "A Knight To Remember," which can be found in the appendix.

"Man Of LaMancha"—(L-R) Don Quixote's niece and Ed Pizzella, as Padre Perez.

I was cast as Padre Perez and, although I was disappointed at first, I came to love the role. The theatre was rearranged and a large three-foot high platform was built in the center. The show was done in three quarters. We played to standing-room audiences throughout the run. Every performance steadily built to an unbelievable climax. When we neared the end of the show, most of the cast had been blocked to be offstage and motionlessly poised at the foot of the platform. When the cue came for the finale, we leapt from floor level onto the platform. I invariably experienced such exhilaration that the leap, which would normally have required some degree of physical exertion, was entirely effortless.

"Man Of LaMancha"—(L-R) The niece, Ed Pizzella, as Padre Perez and Patrique Hurd as the housekeeper.

Patrique Hurd, who had done a marvelous job as Bloody Mary in "South Pacific," played the role of the housekeeper. My most enjoyable scene was our hilarious song together, "We're Only Thinking Of Him".

I believe that this was one of the most well attended and financially successful shows HITW had ever done. Despite the popularity of the show, Dave Curran nevertheless got into trouble with the theatre group because he had paid the orchestra. It had been one of HITW's long standing rules that everyone who participated in their productions was required to do so on a purely volunteer basis. No one was to be compensated. This production desperately needed an orchestra and Dave, to his dismay, found that he could not obtain the services of the needed musicians on a gratuitous basis. Dave had violated the rule and, after the show, was severely chastised. For a period of time thereafter he estranged himself from the group.

I was gratified by the comment in the February 1, 1979 issue of the Newington Town Crier that "Ed Pizzella of Newington gave a fine characterization of Padre and his singing voice was excellent, particularly in the trio sequence of 'We're Only Thinking Of Him.'"

When "Man Of LaMancha" closed, I think I had broken some kind of record at the HITW because I had performed in seven consecutive shows. That's forty-two successive weeks or eighty-five successive performances, including a Saturday matinee.

CHAPTER ELEVEN

MARLBOROUGH LIGHTS
AND A LOVER'S REVENGE

It was 1979 and Ginny had suggested that we try out for some shows at The Marlborough Tavern on Route 66 in Marlborough. This was a old cattle barn, which had been converted to a successful restaurant operated by the Matsikis family. The atmosphere and décor were rustic and very appealing. Judy Poplawski ran the theatre group. She was a short, but very assertive woman, who cast, directed and produced all the shows in a dinner theatre format. During rehearsals, she derived a great deal of pleasure from lecturing the cast on theatre techniques. She would frequently talk about the necessity of memorizing the cues, the lines and the blocking to eliminate any reliance on the script or written notes. She called this process cutting the "unbilibous cord"—what she meant, of course, was "umbilical cord." The ticket price included dinner and the show. Dining took place in one area of the restaurant and, after dinner, patrons would be escorted to another area, where the performance would take place.

The Tavern was doing "The Prisoner Of Second Avenue." I had seen the Mark Twain Masquers' version of the show with Bob Donnelly as Mel and I had performed the role of brother Harry when it was produced by Theatre

Newington. I was obsessed with Neil Simon and had always wanted to do the male lead. This was my chance. I donned my New York accent, auditioned and was cast as Mel. Ginny worked backstage and the director played the female lead. It was wonderfully intimate theatre and I enjoyed it immensely.

When Judy announced that the next show would be "The Sound Of Music," I was excited. I felt that I had impressed her with my acting ability in "Prisoner" and was convinced that I had the inside track for the lead. My confidence was also boosted by the fact that I had successfully performed the leading roles in "Of Thee I Sing" and "South Pacific" and a strong supporting role in "Man Of LaMancha." My only competition for the role of Captain Von Trap was a singer, who had apparently done little acting. I was crushed when he was given the role, but when I later attended the show, I felt vindicated. His voice was great, but he was stiff as a board. A little stiffness in the characterization is appropriate because Von Trapp, of course, is a naval captain, but the rigidity displayed by this actor was preposterous. During the entire performance, he would move on stage as though he were looking for a mike stand and, rather than incorporating the musical numbers into the action, he would stand there like a concert singer. They subsequently lost an actor and Judy begged me to take the role of Franz, the butler, for the rest of the run. I accepted with the hope that it would earn me credits for the next role I might be interested in.

The next show at the Tavern was "Barefoot In The Park" and I was cast in the role of Victor Velasco. I wore outlandish costumes and worked to develop a uniquely idiosyncratic, comic character with a distinct Baltic or Eastern European, not a French, accent. The result was very effective and little did I know at the time that I would thereafter repeat this role dozens of times over the next two decades in a variety of locations. Ginny again worked backstage and a teacher with whom she taught school was cast in the role of Corie. My last appearances at the Tavern were as Avram and Lazar Wolf in "Fiddler On The Roof."

Fred Desimini at his 40th birthday party.

It was at the Tavern that I first met Fred Desimini of Bristol, a balding, good natured cherub, about as wide as he was tall with a booming singing voice. He was a truly comic character with an almost childish quality.

Judy was doing "Oliver" and Fred was cast as the villain. I had dropped in on a rehearsal. They were rehearsing a scene in which Fred was supposed to intimidate the urchins. Every time Fred would attempt to terrify them, instead of cowering in fear, they would laugh uncontrollably. This would send Judy into orbit. She would abruptly stop the rehearsal and, in utter frustration, she'd call Fred aside and try to show him how to frown, grimace and threaten realistically. She'd coach him on lowering his voice to a deep menacing tone. Then, gathering the kids around her, she would scream at them and demonstrate the intimidating characteristics she wanted Fred to display. The kids would cower and tremble with fear and she'd say "Great! That's exactly how I want you to react to Fred." But then when Fred tried it, they'd again laugh uncontrollably.

My activities at the Tavern were interrupted by a run of "The Last Of The Red Hot Lovers" at Matty's Restaurant in Glastonbury. A year earlier, the Mark Twain Masquers were doing this show in West Hartford. I had thought that my success as Van Helsing in "Count Dracula" had earned me some parity with this group and, when I showed up at the auditions, I no longer felt like an outsider. In any event, although I thought I read well, I was summarily rejected and the role of Barney Cashman was awarded to an insider. I was convinced that this was the consequence of politics, rather than any inadequacy on my part.

"The Last Of The Red Hot Lovers"—Standing (L-R), Elizabeth Wells, as Elaine, Ed Pizzella, as Barney Cashman, Sue Donovan, as Bobbie and Sandy Ligner, as Jeannette. Seated (L-R), Director's Assistant, Yollande Michelson and Director, Shakir Hassan.

This was one of the most difficult roles I have ever done. The cast consists of one male and three females. Each of the three acts is performed with a different female character, but Barney is on stage for the entire show. To do this show, it was necessary to memorize the entire script. I later learned that the original Barney in the Masquers' production was overwhelmed and walked out a couple weeks before opening. In desperation, the West Hartford group hired a professional actor from New York. Several days before the show was to open, the actor received a call from New York offering him a Broadway engagement and he immediately departed. The group was compelled to proceed with an actor who carried the book on stage. Needless to say, this was not the most effective way to showcase the art of Neil Simon.

"The Last Of The Red Hot Lovers"—Barney Cashman (Ed Pizzella) lustfully embraces Bobbie (Sue Donovan). Photo from the Manchester Herald.

With this in mind, I was very attentive when I received a call from Shakir Hassan, who introduced himself and said that he was going to produce and direct the show as a dinner theatre production at Matty's Restaurant in Glastonbury. To add insult to injury, we only had four weeks to rehearse. The normal rehearsal period would have been six to eight weeks and the role of the male lead in this show was more demanding than in most. The shining light, however, was the fact that one of the female actors was Elizabeth Wells, an attractive woman who had done a great deal of work with the Masquers. I knew that a number of the members of that group would come to see the show and this inspired me to greater heights. Retribution came on opening night, when the front row was filled by Masquer kingpins, including their original Barney, who had walked out because he could not memorize the script. It goes without saying that many of my most pointed lines were thrust directly at the West Hartford patrons in the front row.

I was pleased with the statement that appeared in the July 25, 1979 issue of The Manchester Evening Herald, which said that "Ed Pizzella is a good Barney—comical; yet a little pathetic. You keep wanting to tell him what he's doing wrong, as Barney, that is," and the August 7, 1979 issue of The Manchester Journal Inquirer, which commented that "Ed Pizzella makes a very believable Barney. His unconscious smelling of his hands to detect a fish smell, his furrowed brow look as the anxious schemer and his lecherous grin all convey the innocent adrift in a sea of attempted adultery. Affecting a New York accent, Pizzella's vocal characterization splendidly projects a range of emotions from fear to delight."

"The Last Of The Red Hot Lovers"—Bobbie (Sue Donovan) hands Barney (Ed Pizzella) a roach. Photo from the Glastonbury Herald Aug. 9, 1979.

According to the July 26, 1979 issue of the Glastonbury Citizen, "Ed Pizzella in the lead role of Barney Cashman seemed a little up tight in the opening act, but relaxed to become more effective as the play proceeded. It was a smooth production, no lines missed, no cues dropped and Neil Simon's lines were as amusing as ever . . . . Ed Pizzella reached his peak in the [third] act with his reactions to the well played Jeannette."

This was really a much greater compliment than was intended by the reviewer. You see it was my intention to appear "up tight" in the first act. This, after all, was Barney's first attempted extra-marital adventure and he was obviously consumed with guilt. He gets more relaxed with each romantic rendezvous and in the third act his anxiety has been subdued by his prior exposure to the weed and the fact that this attempted assignation is with his wife's best friend.

During the run of the show, I was interviewed by Jean Wetherbee of the Newington Town Crier. Her headline in the August 9, 1979 issue proclaimed: "OUR 'MAN OF 1,000

FACES' BEGAN ON A DARE—LAWYER GOT HOOKED AFTER ONE BIT PART." To prove the author's hypothesis, the article included photos of me as Oscar Madison in "The Odd Couple," Padre Perez in "Man Of LaMancha," Marco in "A View From The Bridge," Professor Heinrich Van Helsing in "Count Dracula" and Jacob Berman in "R.U.R."

George and Shyrlee Burr were active members of Theatre Newington and we had worked together on a number of shows. The Burrs became involved with "Harvey" at New Britain Repertory Theatre. They induced me to audition and I was cast in the role of Dr. Chumley. This was my first stint at the Rep in the Elizabeth Kimball Theatre on Norton Street and little did I know that my next contact with this group would occur ten years later, when, having been asked to perform the impossible, I actually did just that.

The Rep was doing "Little Shop Of Horrors." The show had opened on Thursday and Joe Kornfeld, who was playing Mr. Mushnik, suddenly became ill. Bette Scott, the director, called me on Friday and asked me to do the show that night. I did it without a hitch and when the curtain came down the entire cast and crew lined up before me and, one by one, knelt down and kissed my ring.

George was cast as Dr. Sanderson in "Harvey" and Shyrlee played the role of my wife. I enjoyed meeting and working with Dr. Colby Stearns, who was perfectly cast as Elwood P. Dowd.

CHAPTER TWELVE

THE DATING GAME

It was late in 1982 and I was bored. Earlier that year, I had recreated the role of Marco in "A View From The Bridge" for The Little Theatre of Manchester at East Catholic High. Although the show was not remarkable, I enjoyed my involvement because I was working with people I had long admired, Arlene Mann, Barbara Gallow, Tony Valenches, Ed Garfield and Bob Donnelly, who was directing. I had met Bob several years earlier, when he played Count Dracula for the Masquers and Mel Edison in their rendition of "The Prisoner Of Second Avenue." I hadn't done anything in several months and I had developed an itch that simply had to be scratched.

It was about this time that I attended a dinner party in Hartford. I don't remember how I came to be there, but it was an ominous occasion because I ran into Fred Desimini, the cherub I had met when I had inadvertently dropped into a rehearsal of "Oliver" at the Marlborough Tavern. Fred and I reminisced about the good old days at the Tavern, about Judy Poplawski, Louie Matsikis and Billy O'Neil, who, before he became Governor, operated a gin mill on Rt. 66 in Marlborough and used to stop at the tavern after his place closed. Now Fred had his own theatre group, The On-Stage Performers, and was producing and directing shows at the Embassy Room in Wolcott. He invited me to go out there and audition.

The Embassy Room was an interesting place. It was difficult to find. It was located on top of a mountain between Waterbury and Bristol, off Route 69. After you climbed the mountain, you'd weave through a maze of narrow, winding back roads and finally come to a banquet hall in the middle of nowhere. This was it, an isolated, one-story building containing a large open room that could accommodate two to three hundred people, depending on how you arranged the tables. Along side the banquet hall were the kitchen facilities and a small room which served a multitude of purposes. This was where auditions and rehearsals were held, where sets were constructed and where tables, chairs, staging, flats, set pieces and props were stored. It was also used for make-up and costume changes and served as the green room.

Fred produced his shows here in a dinner theatre format. One ticket would be issued and the price would include the meal and the show. The owners did the catering, usually a buffet, and the theatre group handled the entertainment, for which Fred received a portion of the ticket price. Since this was a multi-purpose facility, between events all evidence of theatrical use had to be concealed "backstage." Theatrical accoutrements were rigged immediately prior to each performance and, after the curtain call, were either stored or carted away. This meant that Fred had to hire a firm to bring in and set up the lighting and sound equipment before each show and then break down and remove this paraphernalia at the end of the evening. The actors were expected to lend a hand in the setup and breakdown and this procedure proved both expensive and cumbersome. As a consequence, Fred lived from hand to mouth, literally and figuratively.

Performances were usually scheduled for Friday and/or Saturday evenings. Dinner would be served at 7:00 p.m. and the show would go up at 8:00 p.m. The actors were required to be there in the afternoon to set up the stage, which consisted of ponderous 4'x 8' platforms constructed of ¾" plywood on 2"x 8" joists. These had to be carried from the storage area into the banquet hall and assembled against one of the walls. The set consisted of 4'x 12' flats, which were made by stretching canvas over wooden frames.

Of course, I knew none of this when I bantered with Fred at the dinner party. He conveniently glossed over those aspects of his operation which might be construed as burdensome and skillfully embellished those which were appealing. I later learned that this was one of Fred's outstanding characteristics, he unquestionably had a knack for gilding a lily. Thus it was on a Sunday afternoon in the fall that I laboriously made my way up that precipitous incline and traced a circuitous route to the Embassy Room in response to Fred's invitation.

After the auditions, Fred took me aside and, complimenting me, offered me a role in one of his next two productions, "The Sound Of Music" or "Annie." He said he would leave the decision to me. He was indecisive about what my role would be in the Rodgers and Hammerstein production, because that one had been partially cast, but said that, if I chose to do "Annie," he would cast me as Daddy Warbucks. We discussed rehearsal and performance dates and I said I would call him to inform him of my decision. As a parting inducement, he said, "If you decide to do Warbucks, you don't have to shave your head."

This defining statement provided me with a further insight into Fred's character, one with which I was not at all pleased. Fred was in many respects a very likeable chap, but as a producer and director, he was an up front compromiser. In theatre, compromise is a last resort. Theatre is art and art, after all, is a despotic and autocratic world. You do whatever is required to attain perfection and satisfy its selfish, relentless and illusive demands. You never start with compromise. It's only when you're up against a wall, out on a limb or on the brink of disaster that negotiations and compromise come into play. I must have exhibited my annoyance, when I responded, "Fred, I'm an actor and, if I decide to do Warbucks, I'll do whatever the role requires, including shaving my head and any other selected piliferous portion of my anatomy!" A few days later, I called him and said, "Fred, I'm your Daddy!"

I wanted to see one of Fred's productions. When "The Sound Of Music" opened, I was there. It was done on a platform against a side wall in three-quarters. The show was unremarkable, until a commotion arose when a portion of the set collapsed. I learned that, as debatable as Fred's talents as a director and producer might be, there was no question that in the realm of set construction he was utterly clueless.

When we started rehearsals for "Annie," Fred's hideous propensity to compromise again raised its ugly head. All the roles were cast, except for that of Sandy. Fred could not find a suitable canine to play the role and announced that he would use a child on all fours. I was mortified.

I was always skeptical about how hard he had tried to properly cast this role, but this proposal so repelled me that for a moment I considered the possibility of walking. On one of my visits to my sister's house, I vented my frustrations and cried on her shoulder. She reminded me that her neighbors across the street, John and Betty DiBatista, had a dog that might be available. We went there to visit them and I was introduced to Aleta, a docile, friendly and mature English setter. We were immediately attracted to each other and there was no doubt in my mind that she was perfect for the role. It was agreed that, on the evening of each rehearsal or performance, I would pick her up at 6:30 p.m. and bring her back by 11:00 p.m. When I brought her out to the Embassy Room, Fred and the cast were ecstatic.

Armed with a sack of dog biscuits, Aleta and I made the tedious trip out to Wolcott and back on the evening of each rehearsal and performance. She was apparently unaccustomed to riding in cars, so I tuned the radio to country-western music to lessen her anxiety. She was exceptionally well-behaved, but would occasionally howl, when I was out of her sight. I suspect that she had fallen in love with me. She performed as well as any of the actors, until it came to the curtain call, when she would try to avoid the glare of the lights by turning her butt to the audience. I often wondered about the weird thoughts that must have flashed through the minds of my sister's neighbors during that three month period, when they saw me come to pick up Aleta and later bring her back home two or three evenings a week. "Louise's brother is a pervert! He's dating a dog!"

"Annie" at the Embassy Room. Ed Pizzella and Aleta

The show went up in November and the weather was freezing, but, true to my word, I shaved my head, which required me to wear a hat until the show was over and my hair grew back. I never realized how fast your hair grows. I had to shave several times a day to avoid five o'clock shadow.

When I sang, "NYC," I was blocked to stroll through the audience. At one performance, my son Steve was sitting at one of the front tables and, as I strolled by, I chucked him under the chin. After the normal run at the Embassy Room, we put on a special performance as a political fundraiser at St. Mary's School in Newington. Needless to say, Aleta was heartbroken when the show was over and I was compelled to terminate our relationship. The December 17, 1983 issue of The Waterbury Republican commented that "As always, the little girl dominates the show, but Pizzella was outstanding as Warbucks."

"Annie"—Ed Pizzella (Warbucks) and Kim Chasse (Annie)

Annie with the kids.

When we announced the joint political fundraiser, the headline on page 10 of the December 16, 1983 issue of the Newington Town Crier read: "ED PIZZELLA WILL STAR IN BIPARTISAN BENEFIT AS DADDY WARBUCKS IN 'ANNIE' COMING TO TOWN JAN. 14." Reporter Joyce Rossignol wrote: "Newington's 'Man of 1,000 Faces' will be presenting face 1,001—this one with hair, eyebrows and moustache shaved—when he appears here as Daddy Warbucks in a benefit for the Republican and Democratic parties on Jan. 14 . . . ."

"Ed Pizzella isn't the only Newington actor in the show. Orphan Annie's dog, Sandy, is played by a 'a fantastic actor,' actually an actress named Aleta, who belongs to John and Betty DiBattista of Hillcrest Avenue, neighbors of Ed's sister, Louise Chiaputti. The On-Stage Performers hadn't been able to find a dog, who could play Sandy. They were looking for a good-sized, docile dog, who could get along with the kids. Ed was visiting his sister and saw this English setter, eight or nine years old, 'with droopy eyes.' He prevailed upon the DiBattistas to let him borrow the dog. 'Here I am. I'm a bachelor, right? I go over to this woman's house and I pick up the dog and late at night, after rehearsal, I bring her home, just like a date. The poor lady is waiting up. 'I'm sorry I kept Aleta out so late,' I said.' . . . And a star was born.

As for co-star Pizzella, he first took to the stage on a dare. In 1966, he played a bit part as an Irish tax collector in 'Suds In Your Eye' and he was hooked . . . ."

Ed Pizzella, before "Annie" and Ed Pizzella, during "Annie."
Photo from Newington Town Crier of January 13, 1984.

The Town Crier article of December 16, 1983 went on to say that "[Ed Pizzella's] father was a barber and owned the Strand Barbershop at Main and Talcott Streets in Hartford for 50 years. Ed was born on Front Street in Hartford and when he entered the Brown . . . School, he couldn't speak a word of English. Though he was born in this country, he spoke only Italian. He learned fast and by the time he was at Northeast Junior High he won an oratorical contest. He graduated from Weaver [High], then, cum laude, from Trinity College and was fourth in his class at the University of Connecticut School of Law. He has been a practicing attorney since 1957 . . . ."

The Strand Barbershop. (L-R) Patsy Massacco, Lou Garzone and Louie Pizzella.

"Annie"—Rooster and Miss Hannigan.

"[Pizzella] ran for mayor of Newington. Though he didn't get that real-life part, he has been chosen for 33 stage roles during the past 18 years—in Theatre Newington, Hole In The Wall in New Britain, Mark Twain Masquers, Marlborough Tavern Players, Matty's Dinner Theatre, New Britain Repertory, Little Theatre of [Manchester], public radio and public television. . . . ."

"He is a 'Man of 1,000 Faces' because of the wide variety of roles he plays so well. His performance as the 'crude, course, but lovable' Oscar Madison in 'The Odd Couple' was reviewed as 'the backbone of the play.' According to the Town Crier of April 22, 1971, he 'purred, postured, pranced and pummeled his way to brilliant characterization' as Dr. Kingsley in 'The Impossible Years.' In 'The Star-Spangled Girl,' the New Britain Herald reviewer found Mr. Pizzella's 'fast talking editor was outstanding.' 'Jack of all parts and master of all' was the judgment of the Crier in 1976, describing his 'even, deliberate, dry downplay of some excruciating lines' as brilliant.

He was a 'stickout,' as Professor Heinrich Van Helsing in 'Count Dracula' for Theatre Newington in 1976 and for the Mark Twain Masquers a year later. In 'R,U,R,' he was fine as 'an old wacked-out professor.'

After 17 years of excelling in many dialects, in 1982 he got a part he knew about from his own experience, playing Marco, an Italian immigrant [in 'A View From The Bridge.'] The New Haven Advocate declared Ed Pizzella's portrayal was an improvement on the playwright's own idea of the character: 'Pizzella brought his own knowledge of Italian language and inflection into the play in a manner that [Arthur] Miller himself should not have omitted,' the Advocate reviewer wrote. The [New Britain] Herald said Ed Pizzella 'is the character most likely to be remembered. [He] gives the part a sense of dignity and purpose. His accent is right; his gentleness and old world courtliness—this in a big, strong, working man rings true.' It is not surprising that he looks back over all these roles he has played and says, 'I loved them all.' As for the great reviews, he says he believes in the parts he plays: 'You can't make the audience believe until you do. A real actor is not a phony. A real actor believes 100 percent.'

He also knows the roles. For Daddy Warbucks, he tried to see what he could find out about the comic strip and did some research on the Roosevelt era . . . . The comic strip character, Daddy [Oliver] Warbucks was born into a very poor family and both his parents died before he was 10. He made up his mind he would be wealthy. By the time he was 23, he had made his first million; by the time he was 30, he had earned $100 million. Then he became a multi billionaire. He lived at 987 Fifth Avenue,' Pizzella said precisely. And 'Oliver Warbucks loved New York. There's a line: 'Smell that marvelous Fifth Avenue bus fume. He is also an ardent Republican.'"

'Annie'—Ed Pizzella (Daddy Warbucks), Aleta (Sandy) and Kim Chasse (Annie)

Al Rioux, Newington Democratic Town Chairman.

"Annie"—Musical Director Gail Delgiudice works
with Kim Chasse (Annie) and the kids.

"'There's a lot of politics in the show,' [Pizzella] said, 'including the song, 'Thanks A Lot, Herbert Hoover.' He mentioned that to Democratic Town Chairman, Al Rioux, who liked it. Republican Town Chairman, James McCabe liked it too. They agreed the show would be a good combination fundraiser. In 1974, the Republican and Democratic Town Committees presented a Theatre Newington production of 'You Know I Can't Hear You When The Water's Running' as a bipartisan fundraiser. Ed Pizzella played George and Herbert in that," the article concluded.

In 1984, the Hole In The Wall Theatre again moved, this time to the Italian Club at the top of the hill on North Street in New Britain. They decided to do a collection of one-acts, which they called "Spring Follies." Ted Guhl directed. I was pleased to recreate the role of the octogenarian bird watcher, Herbert, in "You Know I Can't Hear You When The Water's Running." Later that year, I was given the opportunity to display my Russian accent in my roles of the General and the father in Neil Simon's "The Good Doctor," which was produced by a West Hartford group known as "Way-Off Broadway."

Theatre Newington had decided to do a dinner theatre production at Hidden Valley Country Club located east of the Berlin Turnpike in Newington. The show they picked was one with which I was very familiar, "The Last Of The Red Hot Lovers," and, of course, I was chosen to recreate the role of Barney Cashman. The show was co-directed by Mikki Zadrowski and Marge Clauson, both of Newington. Marge's daughter-in-law played Bobbie Michele, the girl in the second act, and Gail Gregory was Jeannette Fisher in the third. The girl who played Elaine in the first act had had very little acting experience. During the rehearsals, Mikki would reiterate one of the basic rules of live theatre, namely that you only move on stage while you're delivering a line. The actress in the first act took this directive literally and she would frequently cause us to break up, when, having run out of dialogue before she completed her movement, she would stand on stage with one foot elevated, waiting nervously for her next line to get out of her clearly awkward position.

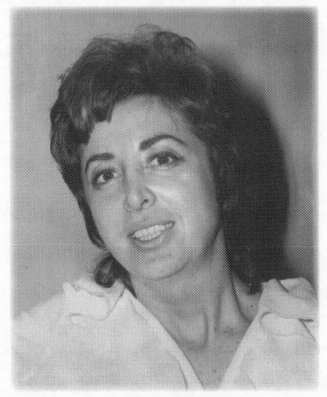

Mikki Zadrowski

In the second act, Barney attempts to seduce an attractive young girl he has met at a bus stop. She's a hippy type and the scene ends when she induces him to smoke pot and he collapses in a stupor. We did a great deal of experimentation to develop a plausible and acceptable substitute for the identifiable smell of marijuana smoke. We tried a variety of herb cigarettes and then I rolled some made with tea leaves. These created the desired effect and we used them for the show. The June 15, 1984 issue of the Newington Town Crier remarked that "We went expecting a reasonably entertaining evening, but it turned out to be a very funny show. I saw Ed play Daddy Warbucks, so I knew he could act, but I didn't know he was so good at comedy. 'Red Hot' is full of funny lines and, as Barney Cashman, he made the most of every one."

CHAPTER THIRTEEN

DILEMMAS AND DEPARTING FOOTSTEPS

By 1984, I had played nineteen leading roles in the thirty-seven productions in which I had appeared. My friend, Lance Samia, was directing "Bell, Book And Candle" for the Hole In The Wall Theatre and asked me and Ginny to audition. At the same time, Fred Desimini was about to do "Guys & Dolls" at the Embassy Room. The two shows were scheduled to run head to head and I was itching to do another musical. But I was also interested in doing Lance's show, especially if Ginny got the female lead. I was impaled on the horns of a dilemma. I agreed to audition for Lance's show, but I made it clear that, if I was offered the role of Nathan Detroit, that's the one I would choose.

As fate would have it, I was offered the male lead in "Bell, Book And Candle," but the female lead went to Barbara Gallow and Steve Liskow, my principal competitor for the male lead, was chosen as stage manager. The fact that Ginny did not get the female lead, though disappointing, would make my decision easier, if I should be so fortunate as to be offered the role of Nathan Detroit in Fred's show. A short time later, when I was offered the lead in "Guys & Dolls," I immediately notified Lance. Ironically, Steve Liskow was selected as my replacement in "Bell, Book And Candle" and shortly after the run he and Barbara were married. I was pleased that my declining the role had brought them together. I felt like a truly successful yenta.

Ed Pizzella as Nathan Detroit in "Guys & Dolls."

I worked on my Big Apple accent and diligently immersed myself in the role played by Frank Sinatra in the movie version. I enjoyed sharing the stage with a number of very talented actors, Donna Kaczynski (Miss Adelaide), Kris

McMurray (Sky Masterson), Bill Cohen (Harry the Horse), Lee Phillips (Big Jule), Larry Osborne (Arvide) and, of course, Fred, who excelled in the role of Nicely Nicely Johnson. Chills ran up and down my spine every time we did "Don't Rock The Boat." Many of my scenes were with Kris and it was uncanny how we seemed to anticipate each other's moves. I knew then that he would some day go on to do great things in the theatrical world and, sure enough, years later he would become a respected director and producer and establish and operate one of the most successful cabaret theatres in Connecticut.

I was buoyed by the comment in the October 19, 1984 issue of the Waterbury American that "As the charming, confused couple whose love surpasses their sensibilities, Pizzella and Kaczynski are cohesive in their stage understanding of each other's roles. His timing and interaction are perfection; with the other actors as well. In fact, Pizzella's precise sense of pacing very nearly carries the play." We put on a special benefit performance of the show at the Knights of Columbus Hall on North Mountain Road in Newington and Mikki Zadrowski, writing for the Newington Town Crier in its October 26, 1984 issue remarked that "Applause greeted the ever-popular Ed Pizzella as Nathan Detroit bedecked in red plaid slacks with matching red handkerchief, red hatband and gold shirt, truly a colorful performance by a talented and colorful personality—my particular favorite being 'Sue Me,' which really was superb."

Two years later, I would recreate this role in productions at L'Auberge d'Elegance Dinner Theatre in Bristol, at the Cedar Run Restaurant in Cromwell and at the Downstairs Cabaret in Newington.

I next played Lindsay Woolsey in "Mame" at the Embassy Room. Ann Brown played Mame Dennis, Fred played Beauregard and Kris McMurray played the older Patrick. In one scene, Kris was blocked to be on stage, talking to his aunt on a telephone. The prop phone was missing, so Kris improvised by holding a shoe up to his ear. This convinced me that he had a brilliant future ahead of him in showbiz. The show required a quantity of edible, but odd looking hors d'oeuvres, which were tediously prepared prior to each performance. When the show went up, it invariably occurred that many of the edibles were missing. It was later discovered that Fred was the culprit.

I was intrigued by the show's storyline and, in particular, by Mame's credo, "Life is a banquet and most poor sons-of-bitches are starving to death." In 1997 I entered a poetry contest. The rules required each entrant to submit an original poem about exotic foods. I immediately flashed back to Mame's credo and penned a poem entitled "Vital Vittles," which can be found in the appendix.

Several days before the show was scheduled to open, we lost the actress who was playing the role of Sally Cato. We were desperate. Fred called Melody Casale. She was amazing. She came to the next rehearsal and stepped into the role as though she had been rehearsing with us from the very beginning. From the first moment I saw her on stage, I was overwhelmed by her acting ability.

Fred's next show was Neil Simon's "Barefoot In The Park" and I was flabbergasted when he gave me the job of directing it. Fred could get by directing musicals because this genre lacks dramatic continuity and plausibility. He studied music and could stage production numbers, but when it came to Neil Simon's intricate dialogue and comic interpretation and timing, he was at a loss. I was thrilled with the idea of directing my first three-act comedy and little did I know that this was just the first of many more versions of this show, which I would direct and perform in. Such replays would occur in the future at the Yankee Silversmith in Wallingford, the Ramada Dinner Theatre in New Britain, the Farmington Marriott, the Bradley Sheraton and the Beckley Dinner Theatre and Connecticut Cabaret Theatre in Berlin.

My first hurdle was to pick a cast. Thank God this was not a local community theatre group. I was not prohibited from precasting and I was not required to consult with a casting committee. I, of course, would take the role of Victor Velasco. I cast Gail Gregory in the role of Ethel Banks, Larry Osborne as the delivery man and Kris McMurray would play Paul Bratter. The big question was, "Who would play Corie?"

Ginny and I had ended our relationship, but we remained good friends. I was now dating Michelle Torbick, who was attractive and looked the part, but had little stage experience. I made the unpardonable mistake of telling Michelle about the show. She, naturally, wanted the part. Ginny, on the other hand, had the experience, knew the role and was available. I again found myself on the horns of a dilemma. Should I cast my present girlfriend for the sake of domestic tranquility, or my ex-girlfriend for the sake of art? In anguish, I yielded to what was best for the show.

Michelle Torbick

I had done "Barefoot" at the Marlborough Tavern. I knew the show and I determined that this would be the best rendition ever. I told Fred that we would do the show in the round and that we would use lighting, sound and technical effects to compensate for the absence of a set. Kris lived in a second floor apartment in a two-family house on Farmington Avenue in Berlin. He offered his apartment for rehearsals. This was a boon, because we not only would avoid those lengthy trips to Wolcott, but hopefully we could avoid Fred's well intended, but counterproductive meddling.

Early in the rehearsals hostility developed between me and Ginny, when I reprimanded her for paraphrasing her lines. I had done a lot of Neil Simon and had acquired a profound respect for his brand of humor. I insisted that the wording be exactly as written in the script. She would indignantly snap back, "What's the difference? It means the same thing!" Then I'd stop the rehearsal and explain that with other playwrights it is possible to successfully paraphrase, but not so with Neil Simon. He deals in precise, cryptic one-liners and he continually makes use of puns, alliteration and repetition. Substituting synonyms will frequently destroy both the rhythm and humor of his intricate and ingenious dialogue. Once the ground rules were established, harmony was restored.

"Barefoot" is a story about a newly married couple, who take up residence in a tiny fifth floor walk-up apartment in New York City. The show opens with the entrance of a happy and exhilarated newly wed, Corie Bratter, who anxiously awaits the arrival of her husband to whom she will joyfully reveal their love nest. Paul has not yet seen the apartment and is stressed out by its diminutive size, its deplorable condition, the high rent and lack of heat, the peculiar neighbors and, particularly, by the exhausting climb, which the author uses as the focus of much of the play's humor. I decided to start the show with the sound of footsteps in the empty stairway.

I brought a tape recorder to the first rehearsal and we spent hours taping footsteps in the stairway leading to Kris' apartment. A reverb was used for the echo effect. We taped Ginny briskly charging up the stairs. We taped Kris climbing the stairs, first at a normal pace and gradually slowing down to an erratic stumbling. Then we taped him, huffing and puffing, as he strenuously carried Gail up the stairs. We taped Gail and the elderly delivery man exhaustively plodding their way up and down the stairs and I was taped effortlessly gliding up the stairs. When the tapes were edited, the effects were astounding.

My plan was as follows. When the dinner is concluded, there would be the standard announcement. The music would come up, as the house lights slowly dim to black. In the blackout the music fades and up come street sounds followed by the sounds of a closing door and Corie's exaggerated, fast paced footsteps, echoing in the empty stairwell. The stage lights slowly come up as the sound fades and a beaming Corie dashes up the three steps leading to the center platform, admiring every nook and cranny of her "lavish" love nest. This would be an awesome opening.

Donna Kaczynski and her boyfriend, Danny Ringrose, were regular performers at the dinner theatre. They had started their own entertainment enterprise and had made a tape of their music, which they asked Fred to play during intermission, as a promo for their new venture. The tape had been given to the sound technician. He apparently confused this with our sound effects tape and, to the utter chagrin of the entire cast, instead of the sound of footsteps, "Barefoot" opened to the melodic, but incongruous and patently unwelcome vocals of Donna and Danny. Pandemonium ensued and opening night was a disaster. The original sound effects tape was never found and all the effects had to be re-recorded, but in every performance thereafter Corie's entrance, accompanied by those suggestive footsteps, was greeted with thundering applause.

After this bumpy start, the show was a tremendous success and the February 12, 1985 issue of the Waterbury American reported that "'Barefoot In The Park' has been assayed by all kinds of professional, semi-professional and amateur theatre organizations with varying results. Although we have seen this show many times and in many places, the cast directed by Ed Pizzella need take a back seat to no one . . . . Pizzella has all the attributes of a natural comedian. He's the best 'Victor Velasco' we have yet seen." We later reproduced the show in a proscenium format for the Berlin Repertory Theatre at Berlin High School.

Larry Osborne

After we had completed the run, I received a call from Larry Osborne. He was working on a TV movie with Hilltop Productions and they were looking for actors. The company was based in Litchfield and they were producing films about youth in crisis. Their films were being aired on Connecticut Public Television channels.

Town Crier photo, Aug. 9, 1985. (L-R) Front row—Brian Ashe, an
actor, Ron Gould, producer, Gail Gregory, actress. Standing—
Rick Doyle, director-writer and Ed Pizzella, actor.

Hilltop was working on a film entitled "Vows." This was
a movie about a young man in his late teens, wrestling with
the difficult decision of whether or not to give up worldly
pleasures and enter the priesthood. The leading role was
being played by Frank Bump, a brilliant young actor from
New York. Rick Doyle was one of Hilltop's principals and did
much of the directing, as well as the script writing, camera
work and editing. He was also a teacher in a private school in
Litchfield. Larry was cast as the leading character's father and
Ginny Vilcinskas was playing the role of the boy's girlfriend.
We made contact with the group and Melody was cast as the
mother and I was cast as Father Brannigan, both supporting
roles.

Film making was entirely new to me and I was fascinated
with the differences between this creative process and live

theatre. The multitude of cryptic scenes were filmed in a variety of places. We shot scenes at Rick Doyle's school in Litchfield, at private homes in the Hartford area, at St. Joseph's Cathederal in Hartford, at St. Thomas' Seminary in Bloomfield and even at a cemetery in upstate New York.

I was amazed by the fact that hundreds of scenes were filmed out of sequence and then, from this chaotic hodgepodge, the disjointed pieces were edited and reassembled to form a concise and coherent media product. I got a jolt out of one scene that was filmed in the cafeteria at St. Thomas' Seminary. The main character had come to seek Fr. Brannigan's advice with regard to his momentous decision and I had invited him to have lunch with me and one of my associates. The actor who was playing the role of my associate never showed. We waited and waited and finally, when we could wait no longer, Rick decided to film the scene without the other actor and we left his chair vacant. Rick later filmed the other actor alone. When the film was edited, you would never have known that the missing actor was not there with us at the original shooting.

Larry Osborne was having a problem with his lines and the number of takes became burdensome, so Rick rewrote the ending and arranged for the leading character's father to die of a heart attack. As a result of this change, another emotional scene was added in which the family gathered in mourning at the cemetery after the funeral,

In the meantime, Frank Bump had returned to New York and, because of his tight schedule, this scene had to be filmed close to the school he was attending. To accommodate him, the cast agreed to drive to New York on a Sunday afternoon and film the scene there. After picking up Frank, we drove to a nearby cemetery on a grassy hill along an interstate highway. It was a beautiful day. The cameras were positioned and in the bright afternoon sun we filmed the final scenes. The crew was gathering up the equipment and preparing to leave, when suddenly the director became frantic and called for an immediate halt. As we were leaving, he looked back and what he saw threw him into a state of panic. The inscriptions on the headstones clearly indicated that this was a Jewish cemetery. There was no time to look for a more appropriate location, so the blocking was changed and the scenes were filmed again. This time, only the backs of the headstones were visible.

After most of the camera work and editing had been done, Rick invited the cast to his office to view the product. I was amazed to learn that some eighteen hours of film had been edited to produce a show that ran for less than one hour. The cast was thrilled when several months later it was aired on CPTV.

CHAPTER FOURTEEN

HE WHO LAUGHS LAST . . .

"The Best Little Whorehouse In Texas"—(L-R) Al Percoski, as the Governor, Melody Pizzella, as Miss Mona and Ed Pizzella, as Sheriff Ed Earl Dodd.

"Awright Gov'nor. All ya had to do was ask." My voice sounded calm enough, but "all ya had to do was" look to know that Sheriff Ed Earl Dodd was anything but calm. As a matter of fact, this innocent sounding phone conversation represented the climax of one of the most perplexing challenges this honorable Southern gentleman had ever encountered. "We'd a handled this thang locally, if y'all hadn't let it get on **Channel 8 Action News** . . . . ." I was interrupted by a deluge of deafening laughter.

Laughter was the cornerstone of my theatrical career. It was there when I attended elementary school, wearing my father's hand-me-down, double-breasted, pinstriped suits. It was there when I did my Yiddish comedy routines at the Brownell Club beer parties at Trinity College. It was there when I first stepped on stage as John Fitzgerald, the comical Irish tax collector in "Suds In Your Eye," and I hoped it would be there at my final curtain call. I always thought of laughter as the resilient, binding fiber interwoven throughout the fabric of my bitter-sweet existence.—No, don't worry, I've got plenty of time before I hit them with the next line.

Ed Pizzella, as Sheriff Ed Earl Dodd receives a call from the Governor

It was 1985 and I was on stage playing the role of Sheriff Ed Earl Dodd in "The Best Little Whorehouse In Texas" at the Popular Restaurant in Southington. Miss Mona was being played by my second wife, Melody Sutter Casale,

Fred Desimini was playing the role of Melvin Thorpe and Kris McMurray was cast as the narrator. The show had opened at the Embassy Room, but Fred occasionally took his shows on the road and the Popular was one of his favorite venues. The banquet hall was located in the rear of the building and we performed in the center of that room. There was a small room next to the front portion of the restaurant, which we used as the green room. In order to make our entrances and exits, we had to weave through the patrons in the bar in the front portion of the restaurant.

The Sheriff, Ed Pizzella, holds court with Miss Mona's girls. (L-R) Joanne Kramer, Sheri Napolitano, Shelly Zippadelli, Donna Kaczynski and Kim Stanziano. Town Crier photo, June 7, 1985

Advance publicity appeared in some local newspapers announcing performances of the show at the Popular. I shudder to think of what the reaction would have been of the Connecticut Bar Association or of some of my distinguished friends and colleagues, such as Lew Rome, Chairman of the Board of Trustees of the University of Connecticut and former Republican gubernatorial aspirant, or State Police Commissioner and former Superior Court Judge Arthur L. Spada, or Associate Connecticut Supreme Court Justice Robert Berdon, if they had seen the eye-catching headline that appeared in the June 7, 1985 issue of the Newington

Town Crier: "LOCAL ATTORNEY TO OPEN 'WHOREHOUSE' IN SOUTHINGTON."

During the show, while I was backstage, one of the actors mentioned that Al Terzi, then anchor man for the Channel 8 Evening News, was in attendance. Al lived in Southington and everyone in the audience knew him. Fred had always encouraged us to adlib bits of local humor with appropriate discretion. I thought this was the perfect place in the show to mention him. My timing was superb and the audience was spastic.

Al Terzi, TV Newscaster.

Ed Pizzella, as Sheriff Ed Earl Dodd, and Melody Pizzella, as Miss Mona.

I remembered what I had been taught about holding for laughs. It was Judy Poplawski who had said that laughter is like a wave. You must hold until it peaks and, when it starts to break, you come in with the next line. If you wait too long, there's white space and that's taboo. It destroys the rhythm and pacing of the performance. If you come in too soon, on the other hand, they can't hear the next line and they won't laugh anymore. It's tricky.

Shy decides to join the girls at the Chicken Ranch.

The most glaring example of this phenomenon—holding for laughs—occurred when I had gone to see one of my first Neil Simon comedies, "The Star-Spangled Girl." This was being performed at the Wadsworth Athenaeum in Hartford by the Mark Twain Masquers under the direction of David Young.

It was a wonderful production, except for one problem. At the beginning of the show, the clever one-liners readily evoked their traditional eruptions of thunderous laughter.

But the pace was too fast. The actors failed to observe the theatrical edict and soon, despite the dynamic energy of the performers and the comedic brilliance of the material, the house was immersed in deadly silence. The audience was afraid to laugh for fear they would miss the next line. That experience left the principle indelibly etched in the recesses of my subconscious. After all the work they had put into the production, I can only imagine how painful that stillness must have been to cast and crew.—It's ok, they're still laughing. There's still time for a few more digressions.

Fred Desimini, when he was thinner, with Melody and Alan Percoski.

Kris McMurray and Bobby DiCioccio checking out Miss Mona's girls.

My life has always been pleasantly riddled with laughter. I've always enjoyed laughing and being laughed at. At a tender age I acquired the knack of substituting laughter for resentment and righteous indignation. I guess I first became conscious of its importance when, in the fourth grade, I began wearing my father's altered, double-breasted, pinstriped suits to school. When my classmates laughed at me, I was troubled. At first, I didn't know how to react. I could not change my appearance. Neither I nor my family had the wherewithal to buy new clothes. I had no older brothers or male relatives from whom I could obtain more appropriate hand-me-downs. I refused to complain to my parents. They were doing their best under difficult circumstances.

I carefully reviewed all of my options and concluded that there was only one viable course of action. I'd laugh too. And when I did, it would invariably knock the wind out of the sails of my tormentors. These apparently were the dormant roots of my insatiable penchant to perform.

Miss Mona and the Aggies. Danny Ringrose on the left and
Bobby DiCioccio and Kris McMurray on the right.

Marge, my first wife, and I enjoyed laughing together and there was one occasion, when we just couldn't stop. Hermie Dressel was a friend and neighbor. He was also Woody Herman's business manager. He would spend all week in New York City and come home on the weekends. He would occasionally hire me to do legal work for Woody. He and his wife, Adrianne, invited us over one New Years' Eve and he handed us a packet of letters to read. This was a parody based on the song "The Twelve Days Of Christmas." The letters were supposed to be a series of thank-you notes from the recipient of the gifts mentioned in the song to her generous lover. At first they are polite and gracious thank you notes and, as the gifts continue to come and gratitude turns to animosity, the notes become more and more indignant and crude, until the last is a letter from her attorney threatening a lawsuit.

Ed and Marge Pizzella having a big laugh at the home
of Hermie Dressel on New Years Eve.

I've always enjoyed laughing and I've found that a good laugh not only takes your mind off your troubles, but it seems to relax your entire body and dispels tensions. I developed a distinctive laugh and would easily succumb to volatile laughter. Subconsciously, I wanted to make people laugh

and this would many years later explain my attraction to and
knack for comedy. I would make my theatrical debut as a
comedic character, my first leading role would be in a comedy
and its director, Moe Smith, would introduce me to convulsive
laughter——which reminds me, they're still laughing, so we
can continue our brief tangent.

Newington Town Crier photo June 14, 1985, announcing the opening of
"Whorehouse" at Tony's Place in Newington. (L-R) Ed and Melody Pizzella, Mat
Zadrowski, Fred Desimini, Susan Simao (restaurant owner) and David Simard.

I even taught my children to laugh. I started practicing law
as the Assistant Legal Aid Attorney for The Legal Aid Society
of Hartford County. I worked under Bill Graham, who years
later was appointed to the bench. Most of my work involved
defending indigents, who were being sued in two types of
situations. In some cases the defendant would purchase
a used car on credit and then fail to make the payments,
whereupon the vehicle would be repossessed and sold back
to the finance company for a pittance. A suit would then be
filed claiming a substantial deficiency. In others the defendant
would be enticed to start a "floor cleaning" business to earn
part-time income and, as part of the deal, would be required
to obtain a substantial loan to purchase vastly overpriced
cleaning supplies and equipment. The borrower would fail to
make the payments and would be sued for the balance due
on the loan.

I studied the Connecticut Retail Installment Sales Act and developed a Motion for Disclosure that was so comprehensive that, as soon as I filed it, the action would come to a screeching halt and eventually fade away. Many of the banks and finance companies that made the loans in these cases were represented by Schatz & Schatz, a large Hartford law firm. After I had prevailed in a number of these cases, I received a call from Arthur Schatz, one of the firm's senior partners. He invited me to come up and talk to him about joining his firm. He said he was receiving complaints from lenders he represented about his firm's inability to collect what was owed and he just couldn't afford to have me out there as an opponent. I joined the firm and, being the new kid on the block, I was assigned the cases that no one else wanted to handle.

As a result of the Hartford circus fire back in the mid 1940's, stringent safety regulations were enacted governing circus operations in Connecticut. The H. P. Hood Company, whose main office was in Boston, had embarked upon a national advertising campaign and had engaged the Mills Bros. Circus to travel about the country promoting its products. Hood's attorneys in Boston engaged Schatz & Schatz to represent their client's interests, while the circus was in Connecticut. This outfit had been in the state a few years earlier and had committed a number of violations, for which a warrant had been issued. The owner was reputed to be a foul-mouthed, cantankerous, rough and tumble character, who had absolutely no respect for authority. Needless to say the assignment was gleefully passed on to me and I was instructed to stick to the circus owner like glue from the instant he entered the state to the moment he left. This, I'm now convinced, was designed to be a test of my legal competence, my improvisational skills and my tenacity.

I checked all the pertinent state statutes and regulations, filed for the necessary permits and arranged to meet the circus as soon as it entered the state. From the moment I met the owner, it was apparent that his reputation was not at all exaggerated. A burley, no nonsense, six foot four State Police officer was assigned to make the inspections. As soon as I saw him, I recognized the potential for catastrophe. The officer was there continuously from the moment the circus commenced operating in the morning to the time the doors closed each night. Every time he went over to talk to the owner, I would rush over and stand between them. When the officer would question some aspect of the operation, I would immediately push the owner to the side and discretely slide my hand over his mouth, as I attempted to pacify and counsel him. This was the only way I could head off disaster.

The circus had a scheduled stop in Windsor Locks. Since this wasn't very far from home, I decided to bring with me my eldest sons, Rick and Steve, who were then five and six years old. I bought them two large boxes of popcorn and took them to see the elephants. They were thrilled and Steve wanted to share his popcorn with one of the big fellows. I opened the box for him and he took some of the popcorn in his left hand, which he then gingerly offered to the massive pachyderm. In the blink of an eye, the elephant's trunk scooped up the box he was holding in his right hand and in one gulp instantly devoured container and contents. The amazed and confused look in my sons' eyes is an image I'll never forget and, try as I might, I could not contain my outburst of uproarious laughter.—It's ok, they're still laughing.

Even when I was a member of the audience, my laugh was so distinctive that it was frequently recognized by acquaintances of mine who might be on stage or backstage. It so buoyed the cast that I would invariably be offered tickets and invited to return. There was one occasion, however, when my boisterous laugh almost destroyed my relationship with some dear friends of mine.

Shirley Miller

I had been divorced from my second wife, Mel, and Shirley Miller and I had just started dating. Kris McMurray, a producer and director whom I had known for many years and with whom I had participated in a number of theatrical enterprises, had gathered an entourage to attend a production at the Downtown Cabaret in Bridgeport. I had gone there on a number of occasions in the past and was seldom disappointed. To me, this was off-Broadway. There were six of us in the group, Kris and his friend, Jamie, Kris' mother, Barbara, his stepfather, Jim, and Shirley and I. The show was Alan Sherman's 60's hit, "Hello Muddah, Hello Faddah."

Jamie Bik (now a successful theatrical agent in NYC) and Kris McMurray

The theatre was unpretentious and marvelously intimate and informal. It was a heavily subsidized "urban" theatre and thus employed equity actors from New York City. This explains the high quality of its productions. In the lobby they sold non-alcoholic beverages and snacks and the audience was invited to bring in edibles, which could be consumed at their tables during the performance. Our table was down right in the front row.

Jim and Barbara Norman.

I thoroughly enjoyed the show. Its humor is based on the peculiar mores and idiosyncrasies that permeated my youth. It wasn't just nostalgia, it was my nostalgia. The show brought back fond memories of the fun we had with ethnic humor at the parties we held in the basement of the Brownell Club on the Trinity College Campus in Hartford. Brownell was a club for the off-campus nerds. Many of the Hartford area students lived at home and couldn't afford to join a fraternity, so the college administration, in an effort to create some semblance of equality, permitted us to use as a clubhouse an old, abandoned two-story house that was located on campus and had fallen into disrepair. We off-campus dudes got together and formed the Brownell Club, named after Bishop Brownell, who was the school's founder. The frat houses were located on the periphery of the campus, so they could do a lot of things we couldn't. Although we were somewhat restricted, we were allowed to have beer parties. And did we have beer parties?

The upstairs was used as a dorm and the fellows who lived there were responsible for the general upkeep of the building and grounds. The main floor was used as a lounge for the members. Here students would hang out between classes. In those days it was an all male school. If you dropped in during the day, you'd find guys studying, engaged in animated philosophical discussions, eating a brown-bag lunch or avidly playing bridge or pinochle. Walt McMahon and I won the pinochle tournament.

Not long after the club was organized, it was decided that we needed a place to hold our beer parties. We got a crew together and worked our tails off fixing up the basement as a rec hall. It was my idea. I had watched my father work with his hands and I knew just what to do. We put up a sheetrock ceiling, sealed and painted the concrete walls, painted a checkerboard pattern on the floor, installed a homemade version of indirect lighting and constructed a massive wooden bar. The Club appointed an entertainment committee, which was responsible for producing a variety show at each party.

Joel Weinberg was usually the emcee. Bill Sepaylia would do magic tricks. Dick Welch would line up a quartet to sing "The Sweetheart Of Sigma-Chi," and, because I was good with dialects, I would do a comedy routine, using a Yiddish accent. I sounded a lot like Mr. Kitzel, a character on the Jack Benny radio show. I had learned some Yiddish from my father, who picked it up from his customers in the barbershop, many of whom were Jewish lawyers and doctors. Try to imagine a diminutive, Danny DeVito-like, animated, gesticulating tonsorial artist spouting Yiddish with an unmistakable Italian accent. That was my dad.

And not all of the entertainment took place inside at the parties. One of the funniest routines was the "Austin-Healey" caper. One of the members of the club owned this petit English sports car, which was parked near the clubhouse during most of the parties. On one occasion, a group of members sneaked outside. They measured the length of the car and found two trees exactly this distance apart. They then picked up the car and placed in between the two trees. At the end of the festivities, the conspirators became convulsive with laughter, as they watched the tipsy sports car owner come out, locate his vehicle and try to figure out how to extricate it, so that he could go home.—It's ok, the laughter hasn't yet peaked.

Sherman's parodies were hilarious. The audience laughed hysterically throughout the show. Then came the routine about Harry Lewis, a deceased garment worker, who for many years had been the productive backbone of the Roth Fabric Company.

One of the actors reads the two line obituary and becomes so incensed by its stark and unemotional brevity and simplicity that he exhorts the entire cast to exuberantly belt out a song whose lyrics are unfamiliar, but whose music commands universal recognition. The house erupts as, to the proud and bombastic strains of "The Battle Hymn Of The Republic," the cast sings "**Glory! Glory! Harry Lewis!** . . . **Glory! Glory! Harry Lewis!** . . ."

I started laughing uncontrollably. Then they get to the line, "**He hath trampled down the vintage where the drapes of Roth are stored.**" At this point, I lost all my inhibitions, all semblance of societal restraint. I was doomed.

My bellows would have made those uttered by Moe Smith at the rehearsal of "Never Too Late" in 1967 seem like impotent whimpers. It was impossible for me to contain myself. I was in agony, but the earthshaking guffaws continued long after the rest of the audience had acquiesced to silence, and their tranquility caused my laughter to appear even more tumultuous. I just couldn't stop laughing.

My companions, joyous a moment earlier, were now horrified. The audience turned and stared at me in awe.

The actors became mute and stopped in their tracks, as I continued to roar. Finally, the leading actor looked in my direction and said with a smile, "Take your time. We'll be happy to wait for you." Tears were pouring down my face. Time seemed to stand still. I was in acute physical pain and flushed with embarrassment. At last, I caught my breath and became tacit and the performance resumed.

I thought Shirley and my friends would never speak to me again. I found that they were much more tolerant of my foibles than I had a right to expect them to be. But when we left the theatre, I couldn't help think of how wonderful those actors must have felt, despite the awkwardness of the situation. I know that, if I had been on stage under those circumstances, that incident would have provided me with a tale I would proudly relate time after time to my grandchildren.—Oh, my God! They've just stopped laughing and now they're applauding. There's still time for a few more reflections.

I've always taken pride in the explosive, and yet contagious, power of my abundant "risibles." "What are 'risibles?'" you ask. Good question. If you look the word up in the dictionary, you'll find it classified as an adjective. I've used it here as a noun. If you search for it in an encyclopedia of anatomical terms, you won't find it. I believe it may have been coined as a noun by my Weaver High School Latin teacher, Gretchen Harper.—It's ok, they're still applauding.

I'll never forget that sadistic, authoritarian pedagogue. She had contrived and successfully implemented the most psychologically oppressive and fear-driven method of teaching Latin that could ever be conceived. She was brutal and derived immense satisfaction from goading, tricking, manipulating and terrifying her students, but she did it all in an erudite and non-physical manner.

She would assign homework and insist that each student be fully prepared to participate the next day in class discussions. Now, everybody, no matter how conscientious, wants to occasionally have the luxury of taking a school night off and skipping his homework. Some teachers would call upon students who raised their hands. Others would call upon their students in alphabetical order, or use a system of rotation in which, if you were called on today, you knew you would be safe until the next round came up and, in the meantime, you could occasionally goof off with impunity.

Not so with Miss Harper. She used a card system. She would place each student's name on a 3"x5" index card. Then, with a smug expression on her face, she would stand at the door of her classroom and, as we filed in, she would gleefully shuffle the cards. Gripped with terror, we entered, knowing that we would be selected at random.—I'm still holding and now they've started laughing again.

She used the same type of chicanery with respect to written quizzes. At the front of the room, behind her desk, was a blackboard which ran the entire width of the classroom. Above the blackboard was a map on a roller that could be pulled down like a window shade. When a teacher wished to torment his or her students with a sneak quiz, he or she would, before class, write the questions on the blackboard and then pull down the map to conceal them. When you walked into the classroom and saw the map pulled down, you knew you were under attack. If you walked in and the map was rolled up, you breathed a sigh of relief.

Miss Harper made sure that the map was always pulled down, even though there might be nothing behind it. She always kept the pressure at a high pitch. There was never any lull. When she called on you, if you didn't stand, she'd say, "Surge," (pronounced "sir-gay"). And if you hesitated or looked at her questioningly, she'd add, "Stand and you may be inspired." "Surge," in Latin means "stand."

When she did spring a sneak test on her students, it was always at the end of the class period. You'd sit there filled with anxiety, desperately wondering if there was anything written on the blackboard behind that damned map. You'd look nervously at the clock and recite a prayer under your breath. At five minutes before the bell, she'd abruptly stop the proceedings, walk over to the map, roll it up and in a high pitched, creaking voice proclaim, "Now you'll pay for your sins of omission and commission!"—Keep calm! They're still laughing.

With all of her sadistic machinations, she had a dry sense of humor and enjoyed a good laugh. And whenever she'd laugh, she'd apologetically defend her outburst by saying that she was merely exercising her "risibles." This provided her with an opportunity to explain that somewhere within the human body there must be an organ or group of organs which, when appropriately stimulated, produce that distinctive series of inane, inarticulate, yet contagious, pulsating sounds which we commonly refer to as laughter and that, since she could find no word to accurately describe the anatomical source of this phenomenon, she had taken the liberty of converting an adjective to a noun. Accordingly, she had dubbed these elusive organs "risibles." She was an extraordinarily effective teacher.—The laughter is starting to peak. I'd better wrap this up.

One of the things I observed about community theatre was that, although comedic actors invariably get a jolt out of making the audience laugh, on stage they seldom laugh themselves. I've always regarded this reluctance as unnatural and, when I started directing seriously, I resolved to correct this situation. So, when I directed the comedy, "Everybody Loves Opal" for Theatre Newington, I actually coached the cast in the art of laughing on stage. Years later, when I was reading Peter Hay's book, "Theatrical Anecdotes," which I received as a gift from my son, Rick, I chuckled reading the story of Sir Charles Hawtrey teaching Noel Coward how to laugh on stage.

At this point the laughter peaked and I came out with the next line. This was by far the biggest and longest laugh I ever received in more than a thousand stage appearances in my thirty years of performing and it was one of my most enjoyable experiences on stage.

The Sheriff (Ed Pizzella) confronts Watchdog (Fred Desimini) and pulls off his wig.

It was in this show that I first began to realize just how convincing I was as an actor. Fred Desimini was playing the role of Melvin Thorpe. There is a scene in the show when I threaten him with my pistol and then I actually knock him down. As we were blocking this scene, Fred appeared to be disturbed and I asked him what his problem was. Poor Fred thought I was really angry with him. I attempted to pacify him and explained that I was just acting.

Top row (L-R). Fred Desimini, as Melvin Thorpe and Al Percoski, as the Governor. Center (L-R). Melody Pizzella, as Miss Mona, Ed Pizzella, as Sheriff Ed Earl Dodd and Julie Woloszczyk, as one of the Chicken Ranch girls.

After the curtain calls, I introduced myself to Mr. Terzi and he chuckled about the adlib. The May 8, 1985 issue of the Waterbury American reported that "Miss Mona and Sheriff Ed Earl Dodd are portrayed with complete realism regarding accents and mannerisms by Melody Sutter Casale and Ed Pizzella, their best songs being, respectively, the touching 'Bus From Amarillo' and equally so 'Good Old Girl.'"

I was thrilled with the opportunity of recreating this role on several more occasions for the Downstairs Cabaret in Newington, L'Auberge d'Elegance Dinner Theatre in Bristol and, four years later, at the Centre Stage Dinner Theatre at JRT's Restaurant on the Berlin Turnpike in Meriden.

Ribbon-cutting ceremony for the Downstairs Cabaret at Tony's Place on Market Square in Newington. (L-R) Dave Simard, Susan Simao, representing the restaurant, Fred Desimini, Dep. Mayor Bruno Perlini and Ed Pizzella.

Fred was experimenting with dinner-theatre at various locations, one of which was the Downstairs Cabaret at Tony's Place on Market Square in Newington. When "Whorehouse" closed, he asked me to direct "They're Playing Our Song" there. My brother, Bob, and I had attended President Reagan's inauguration in 1980 and, while in Washington, we saw this play and enjoyed it immensely. It follows that I was thrilled to undertake this venture as my second major directing assignment. Ginny Vilcinskas and Fred played the leading roles and we performed the show in the three-quarters format.

The play is about a song writer, and one of the problems we encountered was the fact that it required the use of a piano on stage. You see, the action takes place in an era when electronic keyboards were not that common, so in this instance, the piano was just a prop. Since Fred is not a pianist, a real piano was played off-stage and Fred would merely fake it. We had to make it appear that he was playing a piano on stage, but, at the same time, because of its size and weight, using a real piano would make scene changes difficult. I, therefore, designed and constructed a stylized frame made of 1"x 1" wooden stakes, which were painted black. I installed a prominent keyboard and this created the illusion of a real piano, but it did not obstruct visibility and could be easily moved. We named it the "ersatz" and later found numerous uses for this prop in many subsequent shows.

I was now beginning to enjoy the directorial role and I was pleased with the comment of Perry J. Zanett, writing for the Waterbury American in its September 27, 1985 issue that "Director Ed Pizzella infuses pathos, as well as humor, into the production and Susan Morants uses choreography that is always delightfully frenetic to demonstrate the workings of the couple's minds. In all, this is a memorable show."

In 1986, Fred moved his operation from the Embassy Room in Wolcott to L'Auberge d'Elegance, a banquet facility on Route 6 in Bristol. Alan Percoski, my sister's neighbor, was the banquet manager. Alan is an extremely pleasant, substantial, round-faced cherub with a great sense of humor and although he had never had any direct involvement in things theatrical, he ogled every show with intense interest. In him I could perceive the latent seeds of theatrical lust, so, when we were about to do "Whorehouse" again and found ourselves without a Governor, I induced him to take the role. Although he had never been on stage before, he did a remarkable job and seemed very pleased with the experience.

In 1989, when we left L'Auberge and set up the dinner theatre at JRT's Restaurant on the Berlin Turnpike in Meriden, "Whorehouse" was our first production. My wife, Melody, and I co-directed and we, of course, cast ourselves in the roles we had successfully played at L'Auberge. Glowing reviews appeared in the September 29, 1989 issue of the Waterbury Republican and the October 5, 1989 issue of the Southington Observer. These can be found in Chapter Seventeen.

CHAPTER FIFTEEN

THE BIRTH OF THEATRE ONE

In 1986, Fred Desimini moved his operation from the Embassy Room in Wolcott to L'Auberge d'Elegance, a banquet facility on Route 6 in Bristol. His first show at L'Auberge was "The Sound Of Music." Here the shows were presented in three-quarters. My wife, Melody, directed and I was cast in the role of Captain Von Trapp. This was my forty-sixth stage appearance and I was thrilled with the opportunity of working again with Vicky Triano of Southington, who had so convincingly played the role of Reverend Mother in the Marlborough Tavern production seven years earlier. I was captivated by the show since I first saw the movie and, having played the role of Franz at the Marlborough Tavern, I was quite familiar with this Rodgers & Hammerstein classic.

I recalled the singer who played this role at the Tavern. Throughout, he seemed to be moving stiffly from one mike stand to another. I vowed that my interpretation of the role would be much more relaxed, without losing sight of the fact that Von Trapp was a military man. As we neared opening night, I was having difficulty locating the boatswain's whistles I needed to summon the children. I was relieved when my son-in-law, Clay Wild, graciously presented me with a pair, which he had purchased at the submarine base in Groton.

The show was an unqualified success and I was gratified by the commendation, which appeared in the Waterbury Republican's May 16, 1986 issue: "Ms. Pizzella's direction is complemented by the superb performance of a brilliant cast. Edward Pizzella is both strict father and naval martinet. As Captain Von Trapp, Mr. Pizzella adeptly fleshes out his role with the valor, strong patriotism and uncompromising honor so integral to the one time career officer."

Ed Pizzella, dressed as the Sheriff, with Errol Williams and Beckley's Musical Director.

Happily, this show was followed by replays of "Guys & Dolls" and "The Best Little Whorehouse In Texas" and I was pleased to resurrect my cherished alter egos, Nathan Detroit and Sheriff Ed Earl Dodd, the latter of which earned me a nomination as Best Actor in an area musical production, according to James Ruocco, Theatre Editor for the Waterbury Republican.

Next came "Pippin," in which I played the role of Charlemagne. I first saw this show a number of years earlier at the Ivoryton Playhouse in Essex. Later, Fred produced it at the Embassy Room in Wolcott. There, Ed Gilleo played the role of Charlemagne.

Ed Gilleo

The technical effects in Fred's productions frequently left much to be desired. In the storyline, Pippin stabs his father in the back, although later on in the show he is redeemed by the fact that Charlesmagne mysteriously comes back to life. Gilleo wore a crown and a royal cloak and was appropriately clad as a monarch, except for the fact that clearly visible on his back was the unmistakable outline of a brick-shaped block of styrofoam, which was obviously designed to accept and hold the blade of the knife.

Julie Woloszczyk and Ed Pizzella on a visit to the Big Apple.

The production at L'Auberge was a vast improvement. I designed and constructed the set and a lot of work went into the technical effects. Julie Woloszczyk of Bristol played the role of my wife, the Queen. She was in her mid-teens, very attractive, talented and fully developed. I still remember one of the most hilarious lines I've ever delivered on stage. This occurred in an altercation I had with my lovely Queen, when we were heatedly discussing inexplicable deficits in the family checking account. We argued about her extravagance and I exclaimed that "Sometimes I wonder if the fornicating I'm getting is worth the fornicating I'm getting." Several years later, Julie went to New York and was cast in a professional touring production of "Hair."

In 1987, Fred and his group left L'Auberge and Mel and I gathered a group of theatre aficionados and formed Theatre One Productions, Inc., which then entered into an agreement to continue producing shows at that location.

James V. Ruocco, Theatre Editor for the Waterbury American, in his column entitled "Spotlight On Area Arts," announced that "Producer/director Fred Desimini's exit from Bristol's L'Auberge d'Elegance did not signal the end of musical entertainment at the popular dinner theatre. Instead, an entire new staff will produce several shows. They are Melody Casale Pizzella, Larry Osborne, Arlene Hart, Ed Pizzella and David Simard." In the same piece, he also noted that "During the last six months, many outstanding musicals and plays have been performed by area theatre groups. Listed below are my choices for the best winter/spring productions, actors and technicians . . . . Best Actor: Billy Johnstone ('Pippin,' L'Auberge d'Elegance), Ed Pizzella ('The Best Little Whorehouse In Texas,' L'Auberge d'Elegance) . . ."

Arlene Hart, Dave Simard, Patty Kaczynski and Melody Pizzella.

Our first project was to revamp the stage. The existing stage consisted of a one-step platform which projected out into the audience. In the center of the platform were two large pillars about ten feet apart. We decided to construct a ten-foot diameter revolving platform between the pillars. This would permit us to make instantaneous scene changes. I was charged with the responsibility of designing it and Dave Simard and I built it.

It consisted of five sections that could be connected by way of tongue and groove and secured with metal locks. The center section was 4'x4' with grooves on all four sides and a hole in the center that could be dropped onto a stationary pivot. On two sides of the center piece were fitted 3'x4' sections, each with a tongue on the side connecting with the centerpiece, an arc on the outside edge and grooves on the other two sides. The circle was completed by two side pieces with a long tongued side that would fit into the first three pieces. These last two pieces were arched on the outside to complete the circle.

The platform was constructed of two pieces of half inch plywood screwed and glued together, but separated by three-quarter inch thick pieces which either protruded or were indented to create the tongues and grooves. What made the system work effectively was the fact that a large number of casters were mounted upside down on a flat surface underneath the disc. A dividing flat was placed on the revolve and it could easily be rotated from the back side.

Lisa Fruin

Shelly Zipadelli

Our first show at L'Auberge was "Chicago." Mel directed and, in addition to producing, I played the role of Officer Fogarty, again sporting my Irish brogue. Shelley Zipadelli of Berlin and Lisa Fruin of Waterbury played the leading female roles. This was a massive undertaking and its success provided Theatre One with the essential momentum required to continue its ambitious schedule of popular Broadway hits.

"Chicago" at L'Auberge d'Elegance Dinner Theatre—the jailhouse girls.

In its June 26, 1987 issue, the Southington Record-Journal commented that "Theatre One Productions has taken over the staging of plays, both musical and straight, at L'Auberge d'Elegance Dinner Theatre of Bristol . . . . If the stock company's maiden production, 'Chicago,' is representative of the quality of performances that theatergoers can expect, the troupe will soon find itself occupying a prominent place among area stage company listings." The review describes "the portrayals rendered by the entire cast" as "superior" and the work of the director, Melody Pizzella, as displaying "a brilliantly comprehensive knowledge of her material and its sources in film, theatre and history." It goes on to say that "From the very opening of 'Chacago,' the audience is instantly transported back to the 1920's."

The cast of "Chicago." Newington Town Crier photo, July 3, 1987.

The Newington Town Crier in its July 3, 1987 issue opened its review by saying that "Dinner theatre denotes good food and a good show and both are pleasantly tasted and enjoyed at L'Auberge d'Elegance Dinner Theatre's premier performance of the musical, 'Chicago,' in Bristol on North Street, Route 6. Edward Pizzella and Melody Pizzella of Newington are among the partners in the productions at L'Auberge." The article also notes that "A revolving platform brought smooth transitions in time and place: from Roxie feigning pregnancy to bedroom and courtroom scenes; from the jailed women playing poker to cues for individualized exit songs and dances."

The Waterbury American Theatre Editor, James V. Ruocco commented that "Audiences accustomed to L'Auberge's past entertainment fare will note several changes under the theatre's new production team. In addition to a wider stage area, neatly locked into place, 'Chicago' utilizes a turntable that allows quick scene changes and eliminates those tedious blackouts found previously. Improved lighting/sound techniques are also very obvious."

"The 1940's Radio Hour" at L'Auberge—David Gardino (Left), Julie Woloszczyk (Center), Ed Pizzella (Right). Photo from Newington Town Crier, Aug.28, 1987.

"Chicago" was followed by a show from which I derived immense nostalgic pleasure, "The 1940's Radio Hour." I was cast in the leading role of Clifton Feddington. Dave Gardino of Waterbury was the musical director and he brought with him a six-foot high beehive radio, which we positioned at the entrance of the theatre. Al Barron auditioned and was cast in the role of Pops. This was his first venture on stage. We tried to make the presentation authentic and Dave Simard and I constructed a 12-foot long lighted sign, which was mounted over the set. In the center were the radio station's call letters, "WOV." On the left appeared the words, "ON THE AIR," and on the right was, "APPLAUSE." Each section was separately lit and the lights could be flashed.

One of my jobs, as producer, was to edit and prepare the scripts for each performance. As in radio days of old, we positioned ourselves behind a half dozen mike stands, holding our radio scripts in front of us and dropping the pages on the floor as we came to the bottom of each page. After the auditions, a few of us sat around with Dave brainstorming new commercials and revising those in the script.

The show again offered me the opportunity to "use my head," in a literal sense. The initial segment of the show is a depiction of the cast preparing for the broadcast before the audience has entered. In reality, of course, the audience is already seated. It is a scene of total chaos, as, one by one the actors enter and search for their scripts and props and the stage manager directs the placement of the mike stands.

Feddington enters in the midst of the turmoil and orders the cast to rehearse their numbers. He removes his fedora to reveal a bald pate, as he rushes around furiously barking threats and invectives. His impatience and hostility are evident and he never smiles. He disappears into his office and suddenly we hear the stage manager direct the attendants to open the doors and allow the audience to enter. After the pretended audience is seated, we hear the countdown, as the "ON THE AIR" sign flashes and Feddington, now with a full head of hair and a wide beaming smile, makes his entrance and opens the show. It is apparent that a metamorphosis has occurred. The gruff and irascible boss has now become the affable announcer and master of ceremonies.

The script for this show makes a number of references to a Coke machine of the era and there are several comical bits involving its use during the show. It also serves to spoof the then familiar musical Pepsi commercial, "Pepsicola hits the spot; ten full ounces, that's a lot . . ." As you can see in the picture that follows, the script requires this prop to be placed in a prominent position on the set. We made exhaustive inquiries and went to great lengths to locate this essential prop. At last, I obtained the name of an antique collector, who was thought to have one. When I called him and recounted my plight, he invited us to his home in Plainville.

His house was a modest ranch inconspicuously tucked in the midst of a sprawling residential subdivision. We proceeded to the front door and the man, with whom I had previously spoken, graciously invited us into what appeared to be a normal, middle class home. Then he led us to the basement and we were astonished. Every nook was crammed with a plethora of unblemished, antique memorabilia of the 1940's and 1950's. The aggregate value of the contents of that unassuming bungalow had to approach several million dollars.

Huddled around the antique Coke machine is the cast of "the 1940's Radio Hour" at L'Auberge d'Elegance Dinner Theatre.

Our host directed us to a corner of the basement, where we were greeted by an authentic 1950's soda fountain with all of the customary accouterments including signs, counters, barstools and soda dispensing apparatus. He gleefully recounted that several years back he had heard about a diner that was going out of business and he rushed there to purchase this marvelous relic.

As we perused the myriad of eclectic and colorful, nostalgic items, we found our Coke machine and our host was kind enough to loan it to us for the run of the show. I didn't know its exact vintage, but the obvious sign indicating that the cost of a bottle of Coke was a trifling ten cents was sufficient to assure me that it would qualify as an antique.

The show was tremendously successful and the August 2, 1987 issue of the Southington Observer reported that "Completing the illusion of actually watching an authentic 1940's radio show . . . are frequent references . . . to the audience (the home listeners, presumably), the studio audience and to local towns, stores, businesses, streets and other landmarks . . . and the use of an applause signal, which . . . invites playgoers to behave both as a home and studio audience in the most comprehensive way possible. Seen against such a background, the most impressive prop of all, a giant replica of a typical 1940's-vintage radio, seems to take on the presence of a pagan idol or real god . . . . The positioning of such a creation at the rear of the theatre . . . serves to further the image of . . . wonder and innocence-filled period listeners huddled in awe around their individual radios in their homes across America. The cast, which includes . . . Jay Brown, Al Barron, Larry Jardine, David Gardino, Dawn Naples Brown, Jim Smith, Ed Pizzella, Kevin McHugh, Lynn Matthews, Joe Shaskus, Jr., Julie Woloszczyk, Joan Matthews and William Langellotti is dramatically, never less than competent and largely brilliant."

This was followed by the comment in the August 21, 1987 issue of the Waterbury Republican that "Outstanding as station manager, Clifton A. Feddington, was Ed Pizzella, who, with cupped hand and strong rhythmic voice, looks and sounds like the real thing. Pizzella is superb as the main speaking commercial announcer, adroitly telling the listening audience all about the radio show sponsors, including a good old-time remedy for constipation."

The Jewish Ledger's September 3, 1987 issue remarked that "Ed Pizzella's Clifton A. Feddington is a portrayal well-conceived and enacted." And the August 28, 1987 issue of the Newington Town Crier reported that "Mr. Pizzella, as Clifton Feddington, is the character of continuity, shepherding his flock of radio performers, one minute telling them they're fired and almost simultaneously yelling, 'Now, get back to work.' Mr. Pizzella, a long-time actor, experienced in all aspects of theatre, brings a confident maturity to his role. He is the one who introduces the radio show to the audience and the airwaves, becomes part of the serial dramatization and delivers the commercials, which are as entertaining as the radio performance."

My wife, Mel directed the next show, "Damn Yankees." She also played Lola and Al Barron surprised all of us with his humorous portrayal of Applegate. I was cast as the obnoxious owner of the Senators. The October 1, 1987 issue of the Southington Observer noted that "Ed Pizzella is the incarnation of every loud-mouthed, loudly dressed team owner/sports promoter imaginable," while the October 8, 1987 issue of the Newington Town Crier remarked that "The owner of the Senators is realistically acted by Ed Pizzella."

Members of the cast of current show, 'Once Upon a Mattress,' Lisa Feivou, and Patricia Kaczynski, with resident artistic director Melody Pizzella and business manager Ed Pizzella, creators of 'Theatre One Productions' dinner theater at L'Auberge d'Elegance restaurant in Bristol.

Newington Town Crier photo, Nov. 19, 1987.

I was next cast as the Wizard in "Once Upon A Mattress." Dave Simard and I designed and constructed the mattress pile. I also fashioned a realistic lyre for the Minstrel, played by Ron Laurence. I contacted a theatrical supplier in New York City and purchased a number of interesting props. Among them were a disappearing walking stick, a disappearing flower bouquet and a palm-held flame-thrower. I enjoyed working with Patty Kaczynski of Berlin, who played the female lead. We had several regulars from the Hole In The Wall in the cast and the December 3, 1987 issue of the Southington Observer commented that "The singing of the musical number 'Sensitivity' was marvelously done by Eleanor McCorkle and Ed Pizzella."

Patty Kaczynski and Ellie McCorkle

The cast of "Once Upon A Matress" at L'Auberge d'Elegance Dinner Theatre.

"Once Upon A Matress" was followed by "The Fantasticks." Julie Woloszczyk was marvelous as the young girl. I played Amos Babcock Bellome, her father, and Roger Keen played the boy's father. I was enthralled with the show's music and lyrics. It was immediately apparent why this show had had such a long run in New York.

"The Fantasticks" at L'Auberge. Julie Woloszczyk and Ed Pizzella.

The March 17, 1988 issue of the Southington Observer noted that "Southington's Roger Keen and Newington's Ed Pizzella are hilarious as the couple's fathers, who have plotted the children's courtship since the kids were babies . . . . [This] is truly an above-average piece of work." And the March 18, 1988 issue of the Waterbury Republican commented that "Bright spots, as always in 'The Fantasticks,' come in the roles of the children's fathers. Ed Pizzella and Roger Keen make great garden schemers, always pruning, watering and worrying about radishes that come up turnips."

"The Fantasticks" at L'Auberge—Ed Pizzella, as Amos Babcock Bellome, the father, Julie Woloszczyk, as the daughter, and Jon Perry, as the wall.

I was fascinated by the storyline, which reminded me of another show we had done, "Romeo And Juliette." I had always loved Greek mythology and this theme of passionate young lovers being kept apart by feuding parents was reminiscent of the myth of Pyramus and Thisbe. This apparently was in the back of my mind when five years later I wrote "Tragic Rendezvous," which appears in the appendix.

In April of 1988, I directed my first three-act comedy for Theatre Newington, "Exit Who." I then returned to L'Auberge to assist in the production of "Plaza Suite," which starred my wife, Melody, and Al Barron. This was followed by a blockbuster, Andrew Lloyd Weber's "Joseph And The Amazing Technicolor Dreamcoat." I first saw this piece at the Downtown Cabaret in Bridgeport and I was enraptured by it. I was utterly mesmerized by the music, which is so melodic and yet diverse, and by its humor, its exhilarating pace and its profound spiritual messages. I welcomed the opportunity to play the role of Jacob.

I was also intrigued with my functions as producer. One of my jobs was to gather up the multitude of required costumes and props. I roamed through stores that sold yard goods and cajoled my mother, who was a seamstress, to fabricate the coat of many colors. I contacted my son, Steve, who is a plumber, and obtained a toilet, which Dave Simard and I used to construct the throne.

The show was an outstanding success and, after it closed, I went directly to the Book of Genesis to acquaint myself with the scriptural passages upon which the show was based. I was amazed to find how closely the storyline followed the biblical text. Exhilarated by my discovery, I was determined to commit the story to poetic form. The product, "The Prince Of Dreams," can be found in the appendix.

When "Joseph" was nearing the end of its run, I came up with the idea of taking the show to Newington, as a benefit performance. I contacted my sister, Louise Chiaputti, her friend, Olga Amuso, and Father Charles Jacobs and we arranged for a special performance at St. Mary's School on May 15, 1988, with the proceeds going to the Children's Youth Organization (CYO).

Newington Town Crier photo. Standing (L-R) Olga Amuso,
Fr. Charles Jacobs and Louise Chiaputti. Seated is Ed Pizzella.

The article announcing the show appeared in the May 13, 1988 issue of the Newington Town Crier. "This show with biblical origins, tracing the story of Jacob and his 12 sons, is an operetta," said the Crier. "'The music is absolutely marvelous and the production is funny without being offensive,' said Attorney Edward Pizzella, who plays the cameo role of Jacob with a Yiddish accent . . . . Each musical number is executed in a different and distinct style. Joseph's brothers dance throughout the audience in calypso style and another number is in a western motif. Added to the fun is a camel portrayed by two people. Mr. Pizzella said, 'It is the

funniest looking thing wearing a Groucho Marx false face.'"
The committee consisted of my wife, Mel, and I, my sister,
Louise, Olga, Fr. Jacobs and Alan and Donna Percoski and
the show was well received.

When "Joseph" was about to open, Theatre One offered
me the opportunity to direct a show that I had wanted to stage
for a long time, "Casablanca." This was a movie adapted from
a stage play entitled "Everybody Comes To Rick's" by Murray
Burnell and Joan Alison.

This was the first show I had ever seen at the Hole In The
Wall Theatre in New Britain. In the early 1970's, the theatre
was located in a small bookstore on Allen Street. Ray Shinn
had adapted the screen play and directed. The sales counter
in the tiny store became the bar. Tony Grano, who operated
the Brown Derby, a nearby watering hole, played the role of
Karl, the maitre-d', and Ted Guhl played Rick. A couple of
dozen chairs were placed in the center of the store and the
action took place all around them. I was greatly impressed with
both the intimacy and professional quality of the production.

It was now some fifteen years later. I called Ray to find
out where I could obtain a copy of the script he had used.
He laughed and told me there was no script and that he
had simply adapted the screen play. He was kind enough
to provide me with a copy of the screen play, which I then
adapted for the stage. Some of the scenes were played
on the one-step platform, which was customarily used for
performances, but much of the action took place throughout
the entire banquet hall.

The piano was placed in a prominent position near the
banquet tables. I was very fortunate to obtain the services
of Frank Rendon of Hartford, a gifted pianist. Frank was my
Sam. We also enlisted the services of some lovely young
actresses, who seductively crooned the songs of the 1940's,
as the audience entered and were seated.

The banquet tables were arranged throughout the hall in
their normal pattern. There was a remote section of the hall
that, because of its distance from the stage, was seldom
occupied during performances. This area was screened off
and used as the gambling room.

I recruited some thirty actors, many of whom, at the opening, were seated at the banquet tables and appeared to be patrons. Gus Engelke of Farmington, played the role of Karl, the maitre-d', Al Timmons was Rick, Ron Laurence was Capt. Renault and Mark Moyle was Major Strasser.

Frank Rendon and Gus Engelke

Karl would greet and seat the patrons as they entered. While he was doing this and dinner was being served, Sam and the girls were entertaining the audience. When the meal was concluded, the revolving platform turned exposing a couple of gendarmes with a large map of Europe, the Mediterranean and northern Africa. One of the officers was briefing the other and thus laying out the plot. The speaker explained the various routes by which one could escape the clutches of the Nazis and announced that it was their job to apprehend the culprit or culprits, who had murdered two German curriers and stolen secret documents.

One of the officers then steps off the platform and proceeds to one of the tables, where he starts to interrogate a gentleman, who appears to be a member of the audience. The officer asks to see the suspect's "papers." The suspect suddenly becomes very nervous and bolts for the door. The officer draws his sidearm and fires. The suspect screams in pain and collapses. Two more officers appear from backstage and remove the corpse. This opening was so realistic that at every performance patrons would leap to their feet in terror.

During each performance, actors were positioned in the screened-off gambling area making the sounds of the spinning roulette wheel and dice being cast and mimicking the announcements of the croupier, "Faites vos jeux!"

"Casablanca"—Larry Osborne tries to impress Maureen Morse, the female lead.

I wanted to make the show as realistic as possible, so I used the sequential airplane sound effects that the Hole In The Wall had used in their original production. We rigged a series of speakers on the ceiling, so that when the plane took off at the end of the show, you could hear the sound of its engines moving overhead from one side of the room to the other.

I also placed great emphasis on the scene in the café when the French patrons sing the Marseillaise and drown out the German officers, singing their national anthem. Relying on my knowledge of French, I drilled the cast on the pronunciation of the French lyrics and building the song to a climax. I insisted that they sing it with the fervor of a true patriotic Frenchman. I passed out copies of the lyrics and coached them endlessly on every nuance of inflection and rhythm. Different members of the cast were assigned different points of entrance, which gradually developed the build. I was successful in accomplishing the desired effect. *"Allons enfants de la Patrie. Le jour de gloire est arrive!"*

Larry Osborne was cast in several minor roles, but became ill on opening night. I was the only one within reach who could replace him at the eleventh hour and was thus deprived of the opportunity of standing on the sidelines to enjoy the fruits of my labor.

I was flattered by the review that appeared in a June, 1988 issue of the Southington Observer: "With his adaptation of the script of 'Casablanca' to the stage of L'Auberge d'Elegance Dinner Theatre, Edward G. Pizzella has guided the creative process that has shaped and brought full circle what many regard as America's favorite movie . . . . In so doing, Pizzella has brought what many believe to be the immortal story of Rick Blaine, Ilsa Lund, Victor Lazlo and all the rest of the denizens of Rick's Café Americain, situated in the exotic and intrigue-ridden Moroccan city of Casablanca, back to the medium for which it was originally created—that of the live stage."

Al Timmons as Rick.

The article goes on to say that "The director-writer also demonstrates his familiarity with his material—and his audience—by his prefacing of each of Casablanca's performances with a brief delineation of the situation in Casablanca—and the world surrounding it—of December 1941. This device not only serves to enhance the period flavor of the production and further the illusion that the viewer has been transported back to the early years of World War II, but also enlightens the theatergoer unacquainted with the history of the era and with the fact that, at this time, Nazi Germany stood triumphant in the full tide of victory, advancing unstoppably across most of Europe and North Africa, with two of the few free spots in these troubled areas being Vichy-France . . . and France's North African colonies, chief among them Morocco."

CHAPTER SIXTEEN

THE SHOW MUST GO ON

"Casablanca" was followed at L'Auberge by "A Funny Thing Happened On The Way To The Forum" and "Two By Two." In the meantime, Kris McMurray and his Candlelight Players were doing dinner theatre at Beckley Gardens in Berlin. It was 1988 and Kris had decided to revive "Barefoot In The Park" and asked me to play Velasco. I couldn't refuse and took a leave of absence from L'Auberge.

Kris was able to reassemble our original cast and he played Paul, Ginny Vilcinskas played Corie, Gail Gregory played Mrs. Banks and I was Velasco. This was my first show at Beckley and I was thrilled with the opportunity of working again with Kris, Ginny and Gail. I was also happy to recreate a role, which had previously given me so much satisfaction.

We used the same basic concept as in our original version and adapted the blocking to the proscenium form. I, of course, worked with Kris to design and construct the set. I spent countless hours shaping styrofoam to create the notorious radiator.

I returned from Beckley to fulfill my commitment with Lance Samia to produce "Count Dracula" at L'Auberge. Lance directed, Chris Ryan was cast as Jonathan, Ginny was Mina, Lynne Anderson was Sybil, Al Barron was Dr. Seward, Bob Dio was Dracula and I was Professor Van Helsing. Although this was the third time I had played this role, it was an entirely new experience. This was the first time I had done the show in an intimate setting. I designed and built two fog machines using dry ice and I also helped Lance with the other special effects, which were spectacular. Lance had a fantastic imagination, which was supported by his background as an engineer.

Lance Samia

I took great pride in my characterization of the brilliant and intense, but somewhat child-like Dutch professor, who had acquired universal acclaim as a vampire slayer. I particularly relished the scene, when, in a fit of utter frustration, the professor desperately tries to explain to Jonathan and Dr. Seward the habits, evil powers and vulnerabilities of vampires. Pacing center stage, I deliver an impassioned tirade, which builds to a climax and, realizing that I have failed to impress them with the gravity of the situation, I abruptly and dramatically exit in humiliation.

Although this was not the end of the scene, my exit normally provoked thunderous applause and, when I arrived backstage, it would take me all of fifteen minutes to calm down. I felt gratified when the October 7, 1988 issue of the Waterbury Republican commented that "Ed Pizzella, as Professor Heinrich Van Helsing, delivers the most passionate performance of the play."

With the close of "Dracula," I was ready for a well-earned rest. This was my sixtieth venture on stage and it was with no little disappointment that I reluctantly determined to minimize my involvement in Theatre One's next production. Tom Chute of Southington was chosen to direct "My Fair Lady." This show was my long standing theatrical obsession. I simply adored Rex Harrison and the role of Henry Higgins. I had always dreamed of performing this role and I kicked myself, when I realized that I had painted myself into a corner and squandered the opportunity of a lifetime. The role of Higgins was being played by a local radio personality and a friend of his was playing Colonel Pickering.

My Fair Lady—Director, Tom Chute.

The cast of My Fair Lady at L' Auberge d' Elegance

After four weeks of rehearsal, the director came to me in a panic. The actor cast as Higgins had quit and with him his friend, who had taken the role of Pickering. It seems that they just couldn't memorize the script. Tom asked me to take the role and it took me all of two seconds to say "yes." Al Barron agreed to play Pickering and we were on our way. Jennifer Graham, the girl who had been cast as Eliza, was marvelous. She was a petite redhead with a great voice and a rubber face.

Tom was the manager of radio station WATR in Waterbury and had brought with him a number of his co-workers. These included Linda Varrone of Bridgeport and Larry Davis, a talented radio personality who excelled in the role of Alfie Doolittle.

Jennifer Graham as Eliza Doolittle

"My Fair Lady"—(L-R) Jennifer Graham (Eliza) and Ed
Pizzella (Henry Higgins) at the cast party.

I was ecstatic and the show was a stupendous success. The November 11, 1988 issue of the Waterbury Republican remarked that "Both Ed Pizzella, who played Henry Higgins, and Al Barron, who played Col. Pickering, put in notable performances. Pizzella made a great hardened Higgins. Pizzella has a way about him that convinces people he really doesn't believe this street waif is a person with human feelings . . . . He does a good job counterbalancing Eliza."

My fascination with the plot never waned. It reminded me so much of "Man Of LaMancha." I familiarized myself with the story of Pygmalion, the mythological origin of the show, and five years later I wrote a poem entitled "The Model Wife," which appears in the appendix.

With the opening of "My Fair Lady," I could at last take a rest. Mel was directing "Little Shop Of Horrors" with the able assistance of Bruce Campione in the role of the dentist and Bobby DiCioccio in the role of Seymour. The show was in good hands and I could now exit the stage and devote my efforts to the rigors of producing.

"Little Shop"—Bobby DiCioccio (Seymour) dances with Wanda Ware (Donnette).

I simply adored "Little Shop" from the first time I saw it at the Orpheum on Second Avenue in New York. I was so impressed with it that I went back at least three times. On one occasion, I was with a group of theatre friends and, after the show, we crossed Second Avenue to a Russian restaurant called "The Kiev." I had been there many times and enjoyed their wonderful blintzes. We sat down to eat and to our surprise at the next table was the young actor who had played the role of Seymour.

Gus, Lisa and a street urchin with Audrey II (the maneater) in the foreground.

Once we had decided to do the show, the big question was "what to do about the plants?" The technical aspects of this production were formidable. We needed four prop plants, a small one that could be manipulated like a hand puppet—this would be placed on a shelf with the manipulator concealed backstage—a somewhat larger version attached to a jacket with a false arm—the false arm appears to be holding the plant, while the manipulator's real arm, hidden under the jacket and inserted up through the bottom of the plant, actually performs the manipulation—a free standing version, large enough to contain the manipulator in a sitting position, and finally one that stands about six feet tall with the manipulator standing inside. This is the plant that, near the end of the show, swallows Mushnik, the shopkeeper. All of the plants were designed to perform a variety of choreographed movements and functions, which included songs and dialogue.

(L-R) Dave Simard (Technical Director), Kevin Johnston, as the voice of Audrey II and Jennifer Graham, as Eliza Doolittle.

When I first saw the show at the Orpheum, I was mesmerized by these incredible props. I was chosen to call New York to make arrangements to rent them for the run. The issue was quickly resolved when I was quoted a rental fee of $2,500.00. Since we had already announced the show, we had no alternative but to make the props ourselves.

We purchased foam rubber, Styrofoam balls, canvas, paint, aluminum tubing, chicken wire and hot glue guns. Dave Simard acquired a tube-bender and we went to work. The two smaller plants were fairly easy to fabricate. The smallest was the size of a normal house plant. It was constructed with a hole in the bottom and a sleeve that ran up into the artificial plant, so that the manipulator's hand could be inserted from underneath.

The street urchins at the cast party.

A larger version was attached to a jacket with one of its arms being stuffed and wrapped around the pot, appearing to hold it. When Seymour puts on the jacket, because it appears that the stuffed arm is holding the pot, one of his arms is free to insert into the pot from inside the jacket and manipulate the plant. The larger two were more difficult to construct. Their frames were made of aluminum tubing. These were covered, first with chicken wire, then Styrofoam padding and finally canvas. Various sizes of Styrofoam balls were cut in half and glued to the surface in random patterns and then paint was applied. The jaws were hinged and ropes were attached to permit the manipulators to easily open and close them.

The Stage Manager with two of the urchins.

Rehearsals went well and, on tech Sunday, John Voket, who was playing the role of Mr. Mushnik, got into an argument with the director and walked out. Mel convinced me to take the role and it was an omen of things to come.

The show drew receptive audiences and, although it was too late to change the program, the January 20, 1989 issue of the Waterbury Republican commented that "A last minute change saw Ed Pizzella doing a skillful turn as Mr. Mushnik, the Yiddish flower shop owner, as he 'oy vey'd' through his 'foins' exclaiming, 'God, what an existence I got!'"

If there should be any doubt as to the accuracy of this account, the question can be quickly resolved by reference to Eleanore Myers' review, which appeared in the February 2, 1989 issue of the West Haven News: "You will absolutely enjoy yourself at L'Auberge d'Elegance Dinner Theatre, Route 6, Bristol. The casting is one of the best this reviewer has seen in some time." After heaping praise on Bobby DiCoccio, as Seymour, Shellie Cicero, as Audrey, and Bruce Campione, as the dentist, she goes on to say that "John Voket gave us a versatile Mr. Mushnik, 'Mushnik And Son' thoroughly delighting everyone . . . . All in all, I was impressed at the powerhouse of talent the cast provided in their rendition of 'Little Shop Of Horrors.' Great music too."

I appreciated the compliment, even though the name was wrong. Ms. Myers apparently devoted so much of her attention to the action on stage that she failed to take note of the announcement that I was playing the role of Mr. Mushnik, the shopkeeper.

It was ironic that in 1989 I was cast in the role of Mushnik at the very last minute because of the sudden departure of an actor and that two years later history would be repeated. It was a Friday morning in 1991 and I was in my office reviewing a file in preparation for an appointment with a client, when my secretary buzzed me and informed me that Bette Scott was on the phone. Bette was directing "Little Shop" at New Britain Repertory Theatre. The show had opened the night before. Bobby DiCioccio was playing Seymour and Joe Kornfeld was playing Mushnik. She said that Joe was ill and that they were sold out for tonight's show. She asked if I would do Mushnik.

I was stunned and hesitated in shock for a few moments. I hadn't even thought about this show or seen a script in two years. I had done the show in three-quarters and this was a proscenium production. Except for Bobby, it was an entirely new and strange cast with a new artistic director, a new musical director and completely different blocking. What she was asking was impossible. I agreed to do it.

"Meet me at the theatre at 3:00 PM," I said, "and have the musical director there, together with any members of the cast you can round up." I cleared my desk, cancelled my afternoon appointments and hurried home to see if I could find any remnants of the costume I had worn two years earlier.

When I arrived at the theatre, I was pleased to be greeted by Bobby DiCioccio and comforted to learn that Linda Stewart was playing Ronnette and Mario Barboza was the voice of Audrey II. Bette handed me a script and gave me a tour of the set. Then she walked me through the blocking. We laboriously rehearsed the musical numbers and suddenly it was 8:00 PM and the audience was waiting to be let in. Bette told me

I could carry the script on stage. I refused to do so, but kept it in a accessible nook backstage. The audience was seated, the curtain was up and I was on.

We performed the show without a hitch and it was spectacular. The audience thoroughly enjoyed the performance, but had not the slightest inkling of the insurmountable hurdles that had to be vaulted earlier that day in order to make that performance possible. And when the curtain came down, the entire cast and crew lined up before me, kneeled down and kissed my ring.

CHAPTER SEVENTEEN

THEATRE ON THE MOVE

While we were doing "Little Shop Of Horrors" at L'Auberge, we were notified that the banquet facility had been sold and that the new owner did not want to continue the dinner theatre. From June of 1987 through February of 1989, Theatre One had successfully produced thirteen Broadway shows, ten of which were musicals. While we were in the process of looking for a new home, I was contacted by a theatre friend, who asked if I'd be interested in taking a role in an original play entitled "Beyond A Shadow," which was being produced by S. R. Trumbull Productions at the Wallace-Stevens Theatre in Hartford. I played the supporting role of David Cook and I enjoyed working in this state-of-the-art theatre, which for many years had been the home of Sal Marchese's Producing Guild.

Jim Brennan, TN President

It was about this time that I received a rather peculiar call from Jim Brennan, President of Theatre Newington. I could tell from his voice that he was thoroughly exasperated. TN was in rehearsal with a old British piece entitled "Outward Bound." This is a show which provocatively probes the souls of its principal characters, who, unbeknown to themselves, as well as the audience, have departed this life and are on their way to final judgment. Having been first produced in London in 1923, it is couched in language unfamiliar to American audiences. The director engaged by TN concluded that the language of the script was a problem and she decided to change it to a form more consistent with today's vernacular.

Cast of "Outward Bound"—(Standing L-R) Mark Moyle, Linda Varrone, Sy Levine, Al Barron, Al Timmons and Jim Brennan. (Seated L-R) Barbara Gallow, Ina Neiman and Guy Camarca, Jr. Town Crier photo, April 14, 1989.

It was now three weeks prior to opening and it had become apparent that her approach was not working. TN's Board of Directors became alarmed and discharged her. They were now looking for a replacement, so that the show could open on schedule.

(L-R) Alan Timmons, Dave Faucher and Susan Thorner.

I held my breath, as Jim frantically blurted out his tale of woe and, at the conclusion, asked me to take over the direction. I told him that I had never heard of the piece and that I would have to read the script before I could make a commitment. He provided me with a copy. I read it and called him back. I told him I was willing to take the project on, provided that the Board of Directors would allow me full reign to do what I felt was necessary to save the show. He accepted my terms and I attended the next scheduled rehearsal.

I was already familiar with most of the cast, which included Linda Varrone, Mark Moyle, Alan Timmons, Ina Neiman, Guy Camarca, Jr., Barbara Gallow, Jim Brennan and Al Barron.

The first thing I did was to eliminate all the changes in the script made by the previous director. I explained that those changes, in my opinion, were inconsistent with both the flow of the action and the author's underlying concept of the show and actually destroyed much of the local humor and satire. I retained most of the major blocking and concentrated on inflection and delivery.

My approach worked and the April 4, 1989 issue of the Newington Town Crier commented that "Director Ed Pizzella has cast a unifying spell over the characters in this play, holding them in a surging ebb and flow of emotions . . . Mr. Pizzella is to be congratulated for sustaining the action, pace, mood and spirit of the performance."

In 1989, Theatre One left L'Auberge and moved to JRT's on the Berlin Turnpike in Meriden. Our first show at the new location was "The Best Little Whorehouse In Texas" and I was again cast as Sheriff Ed Earl Dodd. Melody and I co-directed and she played Mona. It was a thrill to revive my dynamic alter ego and the September 29, 1989 issue of the Waterbury Republican remarked that "Edward Pizzella, as Sheriff Ed Earl Dodd, roams the stage cussing like a storm trooper, much to the delight of the audience. He has a wonderful sense of comic timing that comes alive whenever he is forced to tell the citizens of Gilbert, Texas, 'where to go.'"

The October 5, 1989 issue of the Southington Observer commented that "The 'I do wish I said that' award has to go to Sheriff Ed Earl Dodd, played with fervor by Edward G. Pizzella. Dodd is the ever faithful watchdog of the community and loves to tell about the exciting arrests he has made. Pizzella probably has the most difficult role in this play. Most of his speaking parts consist of rapid-fire, insulting similes. He had the audience laughing so much that they hardly had time to finish laughing at one, when he would scream out a few more."

"Hello Dolly"—Joyce Follo (Dolly Levi) and Ed Pizzella (Horace Vandergelder).

After a guest appearance on Claire Lear Brown's television show, "Good Old Days," on Channel 32 in Newington, I was cast as Horace Vandergelder in Southington Community Theatre's production of "Hello Dolly." The show was directed by Tom Chute, who had directed me in "My Fair Lady," and I was pleased to meet and work with Joyce Follo, who was magnificent as Dolly. The show was performed at the Bicentennial Auditorium in Southington.

I'll never forget the intense exhilaration I experienced at the conclusion of each performance, as I crossed the stage to embrace Dolly. The show was a success and for me there were only two minor disappointments. I had become accustomed to six-week runs and after all the work we had put into this production, it was a let-down to perform for only one weekend. After the show closed, the cast waited with bated breath for the review. We were crushed by C. S. Degener's negative critique, which appeared in the Southington Observer. Realistically, no show is perfect, but a reviewer has an obligation to point out both pluses and minuses. The review was unfair and I felt compelled to respond in poetic form. See my original poem, "The Critic," in the appendix.

Prior to opening, Gerald Jacobs, a reporter for the Hartford Courant, came to my office and interviewed me. In his article, which appeared in the April 20, 1990 issue, he said: "If any town residents are in the audience tonight, when Southington Community Theatre presents 'Hello Dolly,' they may recognize one of the actors. The man portraying Horace Vandergelder, the widower who engages the services of matchmaker, Dolly Levi, is Ed Pizzella, who has practiced law locally for 23 years. For Pizzella, a former Republican councilman and mayoral candidate, 'Hello Dolly' marks his latest performance in a string of more than 60 productions throughout central Connecticut. And it all began on a dare."

"Hello Dolly" in Southington. Dolly Levi and her friends.

"About 30 years ago, Pizzella was doing backstage work for a Theatre Newington production of a comedy called 'Suds In Your Eye.' An actor portraying an Irish tax collector in the play dropped out and someone dared Pizzella to [take] the role. 'I can't turn down a dare, so I did it,' said Pizzella, 57. Pizzella was hooked and, since then, he has juggled the roles of lawyer, actor and community activist. Acting is recreation for him, although, when he is on stage or involved in a production, he said, he is serious about it. Pizzella said, 'This keeps me very active, both mentally and physically and I really enjoy it . . . . It gives you a tremendous feeling of power. If you're doing your job well, you can make them laugh, you can make them cry.'"

Ed Pizzella, as Horace Vandergelder in Southington Community Theatre's "Hello Dolly." Hartford Courant photo, April 20, 1990.

"His favorite roles have been of men, 'who are sometimes pompous, but on the inside are soft.' A father of five, Pizzella allows that there is a little bit of his characters in him.

Portraying Professor Henry Higgins, the often feisty elocutionist in 'My Fair Lady,' provided some of his most treasured moments on stage. 'I admire Rex Harrison,' Pizzella said, referring to the star who made the role famous. 'I love accents. I love the British accent . . . . To me [Higgins] is just a very interesting character.'

Along the way there have been times on stage that haven't been fun. One was a performance in a 'disco-ized' version of 'Romeo And Juliet' at the Hole In The Wall Theatre in New Britain. 'I just remember people in the audience walking out in the middle of it,' he said. 'I was mortified.'

A lawyer with a general practice, Pizzella believes that things he has learned in the theatre have helped him, while speaking before juries. 'I've had clients, even when I lost, feel satisfied with my performance,' Pizzella said. 'Your job as a lawyer is to persuade and there is no better way to persuade than to create empathy. And that's the essence of theatre, to create empathy.' His law partner, Sidney Rosenblatt, gives him good reviews. 'He's a highly competent lawyer, who dabbles in theatre,' Rosenblatt said, chuckling. 'Sometimes I wonder which he prefers. But he's very good at both.'"

"Cabaret" at the Ramada. (L-R) John Carter (the emcee), Jane
Kitz (Fraulein Kost) and Gorden Snell (Herr Schultz).

Theatre One produced only two shows at JRT's, "Whorehouse" and "Joseph," and then moved its operation to the Holiday Inn in New Britain. Our first show there was

"Cabaret," which I co-produced and in which I participated as a member of the chorus. The Holiday Inn soon became the Ramada Hotel and I was again cast as Clifton Feddington in "The 1940's Radio Hour."

Kris McMurray, in the meantime, had moved his operation from Beckley Gardens in Berlin to the Yankee Silversmith in Wallingford and, in 1991, I did "Barefoot" twice, back to back, first for the Candlelight players at the Yankee Silversmith and then for Theatre One at the Ramada Dinner Theatre in New Britain. For the Wallingford production, we were able to reassemble our original cast, Ginny Vilcinskas as Corie, Kris McMurray, as Paul, Gail Gregory, as Mrs. Banks and myself, as Velasco. But, when we were about to open in New Britain, Kris suddenly became ill and Bobby DiCioccio replaced him at the last minute. The shows at Ramada were thus dedicated to Kris with a wish for his speedy recovery.

"Barefoot" at the Silversmith. Ed Pizzella, as Victor Velasco

"Barefoot" at the Silversmith. Corie turns up the heat.

"Barefoot" at the Ramada. Corie shows her mother the apartment.

At the Ramada, Bruce Campione played the telephone man and I convinced Ev Weaver to play the delivery man. Ev had years ago served as President of Theatre Newington and had worked on many productions behind the scenes, but had seldom appeared on stage as an actor. Ev and I had worked on a number of projects involving community access television. In 1986, we founded Newington Community Television, Inc., which operates Channels 14 and 16 on the Cox Cable system.

"Barefoot" at the Ramada. Ginny Vilcinskas (Corie Bratter) and Bobby DiCioccio (Paul Bratter).

'Barefoot" (Top) Ginny (Corie), Ed (Velasco) and Bobby DiCioccio (Paul). (Below) Ginny, Gail Gregory (Mrs. Banks) and Bobby.

"Barefoot"—(L-R) Ginny Vilcinskas (Corie), Ed Pizzella (Velasco),
Gail Gregory (Mrs. Banks) and Bobby DiCioccio (Paul).

In 1991, I was appointed Drama Consultant for Newington High School. While I was coaching high school students on the niceties of theatre, my wife, Mel, had been cast as M'Lynn Eatendon in "Steel Magnolias" at the Yankee Silversmith Dinner Theatre in Wallingford. Kris asked me to help him with the set and special effects. The show proved to be both successful and poignant. Mel was magnificent and at every performance moved me to tears, while Gail Gregory, as Ouiser Boudreaux, provided the comic relief.

"Steel Magnolias" at the Yankee Silversmith. Grace Cameron
(Truvy) and Melody Casale Pizzella (M'Lynn).

"Steel Magnolias"—Gail Gregory as Ouiser Boudreaux.

This is a show that portrays the strength of southern women, who must cope with the death in childbirth of one of their dearest friends. There are six female roles and the women meet and engage in intimate chatter at Truvy's beauty salon, which is next door to M'Lynn's home, where her daughter's wedding is to take place. While the women gather to have their hair done in preparation for the wedding, we hear periodic gunshots in the background, as the bride's father, Drum, tries to scare away the birds, who gather in the massive Magnolia tree in the yard where the festivities are soon to commence. With the help of Lance Samia, I obtained a pistol permit and then purchased a .38 caliber pistol, two .22 caliber pistols and some blank cartridges. I used these items to provide the necessary sound effects at each performance. My niece, Tina Shannahan, is a hairdresser and loaned us some of the mirrors and equipment we needed for the set.

"Steel Magnolias" at the Yankee Silversmith. The entire cast.

"Steel Magnolias" Ouiser Boudreaux (Gail Gregory) makes her exit.

Another show Kris produced at the Silversmith was "Grease." Fred Desimini was cast as Roger and there was a scene in which he was blocked to eat a hamburger on stage. The theatre at the Silversmith was located on the second floor. The restaurant and kitchen were on the first floor. At every performance, Fred had been instructed to go to the kitchen prior to his entrance and order the hamburger, so that it would be available for him to take it out on stage. Unbeknownst to Kris, Fred would order several hamburgers and would eat all but one, as he was on his way from the kitchen and up the stairs to make his entrance. Fred apparently thought that the food was being donated by the restaurant. At the end of the run, Kris got a bill for $167.00 and promptly presented it to Fred, who was utterly flabbergasted. Everybody who knew Fred was thoroughly entertained by this hilarious anecdote.

"Oklahoma" at the Yankee Silversmith. Ed Pizzella as Judge Andrew Carnes.

Kris' last show at the Silversmith was "Oklahoma. Mel played Aunt Eller and I was Andrew Carnes. The show had just opened and we were returning for a pickup rehearsal, when we were confronted by a conspicuous notice from the IRS and found the doors locked.

The sudden and unexpected closing of the Yankee Silversmith in the midst of a production was devastating. This happened during the summer and Kris had already announced the next two shows, "The Best Little Whorehouse In Texas," which was to run from September to November 2nd and "Chicago," which was to run from November 9th to January 1st. Caught in a bind, Kris abruptly made arrangements to move his group back to Beckley Gardens in Berlin and there we immediately set about to re-establish the dinner theatre.

Theatre One's last production at the Ramada was "Godspell," which closed in May of 1991. It was during this show that we received the news that the hotel was experiencing financial difficulties and that the dinner theatre would have to be discontinued. Theatre One had successfully staged twenty dinner theatre productions in Bristol, Meriden and New Britain and would now fade into oblivion.

CHAPTER EIGHTEEN

HOW SUITE IT WAS

Hartford Courant photo. (L-R) Donna Osiecki, Al
Barron, Ed Pizzella and Christina Shortt.

On our return to Beckley, Kris McMurray and I agreed to share directing responsibilities. To make things a little easier, we decided to alternate comedies and musicals and it was agreed that I would direct the comedies and Kris would direct the musicals.

Our opening show was "Sugar Babies," a fantastic, burlesque musical, which had been written for Mickey Rooney and Ann Miller. I designed and painstakingly built the set. Fred Desimini was spectacular in the leading role. Every time he did his Hortense routine, I could hardly contain myself. I played the Candy Butcher and the second comic. Others in the cast included Al Barron, Joann Callahan and Julie Woloszczyk. This proved to be the perfect show to re-establish the dinner theatre.

(Top photo) L-R—Christina Short, Kris McMurray, Susan Netupski and Julie Woloszczyk. (Below) "Sugar Babies" dancers with Fred in center.

The next show was "Plaza Suite," which I directed. I cast my wife, Mel, and Chris Ryan in the first act, Jim Brennan as Jesse in the second act and Mel and I played the Hubleys in the third act. I was getting a kick out of directing and performing in the same show. Mel had an incredible sense of comic timing and I enjoyed working with her. She was as talented in comedy, as she was in drama. This is when I realized that the third act of "Plaza Suite" is probably the best piece of comedy ever written for the stage and, without the slightest fear of contradiction, ours was the best rendition of this piece ever performed. Timing, pace, inflection and movement were superb and we could both feel it on stage.

"Plaza Suite" at Beckley. Cast photo.

"Plaza Suite." (Top photo) Chris Ryan and Melody Pizzella in Act I. (Below) Mel, as Mrs. Hubley, Mimsy, Ed Pizzella, as Roy, and the groom in Act III.

I even added a comic bit using my toupee. I wore the hairpiece at the opening of the act and through the part where Roy goes out the window to crawl out on the ledge, trying to get to the bathroom window. There's a cloud burst as Mrs. Hubley looks out the window and, while she is woefully lamenting what she thinks is Roy's demise, the doorbell rings and I enter wringing out my drenched hairpiece. The rollicking peals of laughter reminded me of those I had evoked as the Sheriff in "The Best Little Whorehouse In Texas" at the Popular Restaurant in Southington.

"Plaza Suite." (Act II) Jim Brennan (Jesse) with Muriel and the waiter.

The windows on the set came from the renovation of my law office at 210 Hartford Avenue in Newington. I also induced a close friend, Dave Fitzgerald, to help us out with set construction. Dave is a very talented carpenter and builder.

Dave Fitzgerald

The next show at Beckley was "The Music Man" and Kris McMurray was extremely effective as Harold Hill. I was cast as Mayor Shinn and Fred Desimini was cast as Marcellus. Others in the cast included Dick Boland, Al Bingham, Mark

Moyle and Errol Williams. Several weeks before opening, Fred left without notice. No one knew where he had gone or why he left and everyone in the cast was deeply concerned about him. We later learned that he had teamed up with Steve Ennis and joined with the operators of the Starlight Dinner Theatre in East Hartford.

"The Music Man"—Ed Pizzella (Mayor Shinn) and Alison Cox, his wife.

"The Music Man"—Kris McMurray, as Harold Hill and Marian, the librarian.

"The Music Man" at Beckley—(Top) The quartet with Mark Moyle and Errol Williams (on the left). (Below) Pick-a-Little, Talk-a-Little and Goodnight Ladies.

Despite Fred's absence, "The Music Man" was a phenomenal hit and it was followed by "The Odd Couple," which I directed. Of course, I played Oscar Madison and Kris was the perfect Felix Unger. I also designed and constructed the set. I was thrilled to recreate the unique character I had originally fashioned some twenty-two years earlier. I enjoyed spraying warm beer at the poker table, flipping the pickle out into the audience and delivering the inimitable "F U" line.

"The Odd Couple"—Kris McMurray, as Felix, and Ed Pizzella, as Oscar.

"The Odd Couple" at Beckley. (Top) The poker players and the Pigeon sisters. (Below) Felix and Oscar with Allison Beschler, one of the sisters.

During one performance, a ceiling tile unexpectedly fell onto the stage. I adlibbed the line: "You see? You cleaned up so much around here, you weakened the structure!" It got a big laugh.

"The Odd Couple" (Top) The Pigeon sisters come to visit. (Below) Felix comes out ot the bathroom and Vinnie offers him a glass of water.

When "The Odd Couple" closed, I took time out to participate in a Dr. Pepper commercial in Greenwich and upon my return I was cast as Juan Perone in "Evita."

"Evita" at Beckley. Evita (Mary Cantoni) and Juan Perone (Ed Pizzella).

"Evita"—Ed Pizzella as Juan Perone.

I desperately needed an appropriate uniform for this role. I went to a Salvation Army store and purchased a second-hand, inexpensive beige sports jacket. Fortunately, the sleeves were short. Then I wet to a fabric store and purchased some dark brown material remnants. Thank God, my mother was a seamstress. She had a reservoir of gold braiding and gold buttons. When we finished with that jacket, there could be no doubt that it was the uniform of an Argentine dictator.

The show was profoundly moving from the opening scene in the movie theatre with the tragic announcement of Evita's demise to the final curtain and I'll never forget the tremendous exhilaration I felt, when I made my entrances, and the crowds would enthusiastically chant "Perone! Perone! Perone! . . ." I was thoroughly impressed by the historical accuracy of the plot and the power of the unique woman, whose life the show celebrates.

"Evita"—Ed Pizzella as Juan Perone.

CHAPTER NINETEEN

BACK TO BASICS

"Barefoot In The Park" at Beckley. (L-R) Ed Pizzella (Victor Velasco), Stephanie Klose (Corie Bratter), Gail Gregory (Mrs. Banks) and Kris McMurray (Paul Bratter).

It was 1993 and Kris McMurray and his group, KEM Productions, were again firmly entrenched at Beckley Gardens in Berlin, having produced one stage spectacular after another. Nostalgia now set in and it was time to revisit our 1985 sentimental treasure, "Barefoot In The Park." Kris wanted to reassemble our original cast, but Ginny Vilcinskas was not available and Stephanie Klose of Glastonbury was cast in the role of Corie Bratter. Mark Moyle was cast as the telephone man and Sumner Cutler played the delivery man. This was the second time we had done the show at Beckley.

"Barefoot In The Park"—The telephone man (Mark Moyle) and the delivery man (Sumner Cutler).

I was happy to recreate a role, which had previously given me so much satisfaction. We used the same basic concept as in our original version and adapted the blocking to the proscenium form. I worked with Kris in the design and construction of the set and I devoted many hours to shaping Styrofoam to create the notorious radiator.

"Barefoot" at Beckley. (Top) Kris McMurray (Paul Bratter) and Stephanie Klose (Corie Bratter). (Below) Ed Pizzella (Victor Velascco) and Stephanie.

"Barefoot In The Park"—Corie and Victor turn up the heat.

"Barefoot In The Park"—Kris McMurray, as Paul and Gail Gregory as Mrs. Banks.

In an announcement of the show that appeared in the Newington Town Crier on April 12, 1993, Doreen Riker wrote that "Pizzella, in addition to directing the show, appears in the role of Velasco, the zany Bohemian who climbs in through the windows and whose idiosyncrasies have earned him the handle, 'The Bluebeard of 48th Street.'"

My next stage venture was as the exuberant Max Detweiler in "The Sound Of Music." I had performed in this show twice before. In 1979 at the Marlborough Tavern, I played Franz, the butler, and, in 1986 at L'Auberge d'Elegance, I was Captain Von Trapp, but Max was the role I enjoyed most. The Captain, of course, is a military man and I was thus required to play him as somewhat serious, stiff and stern, while Max, on the other hand, is much more fluid and this allowed me the flexibility to create a unique, comic character. I also enjoyed my scenes with the kids.

As Max, I played a number of scenes with the Baroness, who was played by the lovely and talented Jeannie Callouette. I first met her during our rehearsals and, when we later struck up a conversation, I was amazed to learn that she was the daughter of my first musical director, Richard Pauloz of Meriden. He had directed "Of Thee I Sing" for Theatre Newington in 1976. Needless to say we did a lot of reminiscing.

"The Sound Of Music" was followed by another Neil Simon comedy, "Brighton Beach Memoirs." I directed and cast myself as Jack Jerome. Gail Gregory played the mother and Grace Goff Cameron was Aunt Blanche. Fortunately, we were able to recruit a very talented lad from West Hartford, Matthew Ginsberg, for the leading role of Eugene.

W. Htfd. News photo. (L-R) James Daley, Gail Gregory, Ed Pizzella and Mat Ginsberg.

I designed and constructed the set. This show is usually performed on a set with a replica of a two-story house, because there are a number of scenes in the children's bedrooms, which are located upstairs. The stage at Beckley lacked sufficient height to accommodate a second floor. I located the porch and back door entrance at extreme stage left and immediately to the right of the entrance was the kitchen. The parlor was center stage with the stairway to the upstairs bedrooms. We did not have enough space at stage right for two bedrooms, so I relied upon my ten-foot diameter revolving platform. One-half was the girls' bedroom and the other was the boys' bedroom.

I found an antique sewing machine in the basement of my office building and we used this as Blanche's sewing machine. I taped the sound of my mother sewing and used this as one of the sound effects. I rigged my antique Philco radio with a tape of a period radio newscast and used this as the parlor centerpiece.

"Brighton Beach Memoirs." (Standing) Ed Pizzella (Jack Jerome) and Gail Gregory (Kate). (Seated L-R) Grace Cameron (Blanche) and Geri Sohn (Nora).

The audience was in the backyard of the Jerome home and the play opened with Eugene, a teenager equipped with baseball, cap and mitt, standing stage-center at audience level throwing the ball at a wooden door located stage-left in the audience. His mother would periodically poke her head out of the kitchen, ordering him to stop playing ball and to come in and wash up for dinner.

At dinner, Eugene does a lot of complaining about the menu. He detests liver and cabbage, the standard fare. Since the audience could actually see what we were eating, we had to make it look like the real thing. Before every performance, I would boil some cabbage and bring it to the theatre. We couldn't use real liver, so I would bring slices of whole wheat bread with the crusts removed. From a distance, it looked like liver and it was edible on stage.

The real girls in "Sugar."

While "Brighton Beach" was playing, we were rehearsing the next musical, "Sugar," which Kris was directing. The leading roles were played by Kris and Bobby DiCioccio. I was cast in the role of Sir Osgood Fielding and I constructed the set.

"Sugar"—Bobby DiCioccio and Kris McMurray.

(Top) Kris McMurray and Ed Pizzella in "Sugar." (Below) Ed (Sir Osgood Fielding), Grace Cameron, Pat Keating and Gail Gregory.

Everyone strives for success, but sometimes success can mean trouble. Kris had no written contract with Beckley's owner, Jack Curtis, and the shows were so successful that Jack was getting worried that Kris might suddenly take his group and leave. Curtis kept badgering Kris, demanding a written contract with a penalty clause. I advised Kris not to accede to his irrational demands.

Kris did a replay of "Steel Magnolias" and I collaborated with him in the design and construction of the set. Then, as a reward for my successful rescue of "Outward Bound," Theatre Newington asked me to direct "Everybody Loves Opal." At least I thought it was intended as a reward, but, after I read the script, I concluded that, rather than a reward, it must have been intended as another challenge.

"Everybody Loves Opal"—(Standing) Lou Gagnon, Susan Sheridan and Marty Kapper, as the police officer. (Seated) Ed Pizzella, Director, Al Barron (Sol), Pat Brennan (crew), Barbara Mabee (Opal) and Jim Brennan, as the Doctor.

"Opal" is a slapstick comedy revolving around a "Rube Goldberg" murder plot. The main character, Opal, is an absurdly naïve and good hearted bag-lady. She's befriended by three evil conspirators, who convince her to purchase a substantial life insurance policy and to make them her beneficiaries. They then plot to murder her to collect on the policy, but they must make it look like an accident. This led me to design one of the most complicated special effects I have ever encountered in my theatrical career.

Opal conducted her business using a little red wagon, which she pulled around after her in the course of her daily wanderings. She lived in a house in which her bedroom was on the second floor and much of what she collected was stored in the attic above the stairway that leads upstairs. Opal had a unique method of storing her wagon, when it was not in use.

"Everybody Loves Opal"—Building the stairs.

The stairway that led to the second floor went straight up along the back wall of the set with a railing facing the audience, the foot of the stairs being at stage right and the second floor landing at stage left. The stairway was about five feet wide and the upstage half of its width was covered with boards, thus converting it to a ramp leading to the upper level. Opal fixed a pulley on the wall at the top of the stairs and through it she ran a cord with a hook which came back down to the lower level. When she came home every evening, she would empty the wagon and hook the handle to the cord. She would then pull the other end of the cord (which ran through the pulley) and thus hoist the wagon to the top of the stairs. In the wall at the foot of the stairs was a peg. She would then loop the cord around the peg at the foot of the stairs to keep the wagon from rolling down.

At the foot of the stairs stood a column, which supported the ceiling above the staircase. Above that ceiling was the attic, where all of the items Opal collected were stored. Up against the staircase at stage center was a small table.

The conspirators developed a plan to perpetrate the murder on Opal's birthday. They would present her with a musical carousel. This would be placed on the table in front of the stairway. They would string a cord from the carousel through a hole in the floor into the basement and then run it across to the wall that held the peg. The cord would be run up through a hole in the floor and attached to the back end of the peg, which held the cord that secured the wagon.

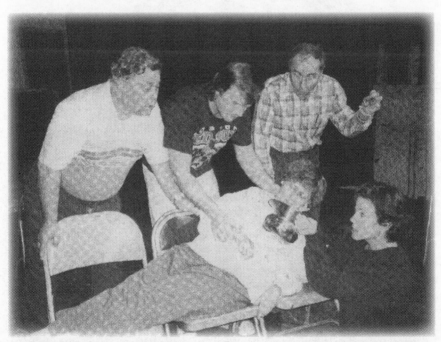

"Opal"—(Standing L-R) Al Barron, Lou Gagnon and Jim Brennan. Lying down is Barbara Mabee (Opal) and at right is Susan Sheridan. Town Crier photo.

When everything was set, one of the villains would call Opal out of her bedroom to show her the birthday gift, the carousel. When Opal would get to a point halfway down the stairs and look over the rail at the carousel, the villain would turn it on. The carousel would turn and thus pull the cord. After several revolutions, the peg would be pulled out of its hole, releasing the cord that held the wagon at the top of the stairs. The wagon would roll down the ramp, striking and knocking down the column supporting the ceiling. The ceiling would collapse, dumping the items stored in the attic, together with a multitude of debris, on poor, unsuspecting Opal, killing her.

The vertical wall above the staircase was hinged so that it could be dropped on cue and, when lowered, would obscure the top half of the stairway. Behind that flat were packages made of Styrofoam and covered with flour. These were rigged so that, when the wall flat was dropped, all of the debris and dust would be dumped out onto the stage. The column was rigged with wires, which could be pulled from backstage to make the column fall over. We had placed a hidden door in the wall halfway up the stairs, so that Opal could escape, when the wall flat dropped and obscured her. We added sound effects and a strobe light and the impact on the audience was phenomenal. This gimmick became the highlight of the show. Dick Michaud, a theatre veteran who had directed this show for another group, came to see how we handled this confusing and difficult stunt and confessed that he was quite impressed.

In my role as director I, of course, wanted to motivate my cast and I have to confess that I was greatly assisted by a technique I had picked up from another director. At the very beginning of the process, when I familiarized myself with the script and roughed out the blocking, I would develop a series of probing questions which I thought might be helpful in fleshing out the characters. At the first rehearsal, I would distribute these questions to my actors and ask them to think about them, as we put the pieces together and added polish. I would also give them notice that half way through the rehearsal schedule one session would be devoted entirely to a frank and in-depth discussion of the issues raised by those questions. This I called the "bull session" and it invariably proved to be stimulating and fruitful. That exercise was always a big morale builder. At its conclusion we all learned more about the nuts and bolts of our project and everyone seemed to gain inspiration.

My Director's Note, which appeared in the program, succinctly exposed the essence of the show and my objectives as Director. I said, "'Opal' is in reality a passion play or melodrama cloaked in the garb of a comedy. It's a clash between the age-old protagonists, good and evil, and, surprise, good prevails. The appeal of 'Opal' is not in the story it tells, but in the telling. It gives us a showcase to display our theatrical skills, to toy with characterization, interpretation, stage movement, comic timing and presentation.

The shallow simplicity of 'Opal's' plot is only exceeded by the depth of opportunity it presents to demonstrate the inherent power of theatre, not as a proponent of good causes, but simply to captivate and entertain. To quote the moguls of the silver screen, 'Ars gratia artis.' As with alluring canvas, 'Opal's' message may very well be that the essence of beauty rests in its utter lack of utility.

In any event, I'm happy to have been chosen for this directorial task, because I can now put to use my bits of theatrical wisdom, which I've acquired as TN's prodigal son, and, with the aid of an exemplary team of actors and crew, we can here breathe vibrant life into John Patrick's comedic lines."

In an article about the show, which appeared in the November 5, 1993 Community Life section of the Town Crier, correspondent Edith Zeldes wrote: "Director, Attorney Ed Pizzella, with a twinkle in his eye and a smile on his face, said, 'This is a chauvinistic show. Its whole function is to pounce upon, jump on and try to kill women, while their female stamina proves their incredible resiliency.'"

The article discusses the main characters played by Barbara Maybee of Bloomfield, Al Barron of Southington, Susan Sheridan of Manchester, Jim Brennan of Glastonbury and Lou Gagnon of Newington and goes on to say that "Mr.

Barron has worked with Mr. Pizzella for the past six years, appearing with him in about 10 shows in which Mr. Pizzella has both directed and acted. He said of Mr. Pizzella, 'He's always put together a very good show—every one he's directed has come out well. He's a perfectionist.'"

CHAPTER TWENTY

PLAYS AND REPLAYS

"I Do, I Do"—Stephanie Klose and Kris McMurray.

I designed and constructed the bed for "I Do, I Do," which Kris McMurray directed and in which he played the male lead. Stephanie Klose was cast as the female lead, the only other actor in the production. The bed, of course, was the focal point of the show. It was very large and occupied center stage during each performance. It contained hidden compartments for the storage of a multitude of props and had a chest attached to its foot. The entire ensemble was on castors and anchored to a pivot, so that it could be easily revolved.

"I Do, I Do"—Desiree Saleski, Stage Manager and Ed Pizzella on the bed.

Then I was cast as Sir Edward Ramsay in "The King And I." Kris directed and he and Jeannie Callouette played the leading roles. This was followed by a musical that had never before been staged in Connecticut, "70 Girls 70." I played Harry and Ann Brown was marvelous in the leading role.

"70 Girls 70"—Ann Brown and Kris McMurray.

"70 Girls 70"—Ed Pizzella, as Harry.

I designed and built the set, including the moon, for this humorous story about a group of senior citizens, who wish to help their less fortunate peers. They decide to purchase the retirement home where they reside and make apartments available at reduced rents for low income seniors. The only way they can raise the money to do this is to purloin furs at Bloomingdale's and Sadie's Second Hand Store.

Grant Brown, Ed Pizzella and Ann Brown.

I had a bit with Ann, which always broke me up. This was the scene in which we went to Bloomingdale's to heist furs. I would go into the fur department of the store pushing a laundry basket in which Ann was hiding. While I engaged the security guard in small talk, she would pop out of the basket and grab the furs off of the mannequins. At one performance, the laughs became explosive when she unwittingly pulled an arm off one of the mannequins, as well as the fur piece.

My role, as Harry, also involved performing "The Caper," which is a breathlessly fast paced musical narration of a detailed, step by step plan to rob furs from Sadie's Second Hand Store. This spitfire comic routine is performed with the use of a pull-down screen, a diagram and a pointer. The bit was exhausting and the highlight of every performance.

Ed Pizzella, as Harry. Dreams up the "Caper," a fur heist at Sadie's.

"70 Girls 70"—Ed Pizzella (Harry) and some of the girls.
Marge Clauson (front) and Gail Gregory (Right).

Fred Desimini and Steve Ennis were now actively involved with the Starlight Dinner Theatre in East Hartford. Kris was still smarting from Fred's abrupt and unexplained departure and refused to consider any kind of reconciliation. The Starlight was planning to produce "Oklahoma" and "Fiddler On The Roof," two shows for which I had a fond attachment, and Fred asked me to recreate my roles of Andrew Carnes and Lazar Wolf.

This theatre was vastly different from any other I had ever worked in. It had formerly been a movie theatre in which food was served during the show. It thus was very large and steeply tiered with tables on each descending level.

"Oklahoma" at Starlight. Fred Desimini, as Ali Hakim.

"Oklahoma" at Starlight. Andrew Carmes and Aunt Eller.

(Top photo) Cast of "Oklahoma" at the Starlight Dinner Theatre. (Below) Ed Pizzella (Judge Andrew Carmes) helps restrain Marty Kapper, who plays the villain.

Steve Ennis had little theatre experience, but, because of his engineering background, was quite skilled with his hands. I worked with him on some set construction projects and was impressed.

Pictured above in Star Productions' *Fiddler on the Roof* are (left to right) Diane Novak as Golde, Frank Calamaro as Tevye, Ed Pizzella as Lazer Wolfe and Ann Brown as Yente.

"Fiddler On The Roof" at Starlight Dinner Theatre in East Hartford. Ed Pizzella, as Lazar Wolfe, has a beer while waiting for Tevye at the tavern.

I enjoyed my involvement with "Fiddler," because I was working with some very talented people. Frank Calamaro was playing Tevye, Ann Brown was Yente and Diane Novak was Golde.

Frank was absolutely amazing in this role and this was the first time I worked with him. I would always break him up in the scene when I met him at the tavern to ask him for his daughter's hand in marriage. The scene was hilarious because Tevye thought I wanted to buy his cow.

Although the quality of Starlight's shows was good, they failed to draw sufficient audiences to survive and soon closed their doors.

"Plaza Suite" in Meriden. Ed Pizzella, as Sam and Jesse with his leading ladies.

The Castle Craig Players in Meriden were doing "Plaza Suite." I auditioned and was cast in the role of Sam Nash, the male lead in the first act. After several weeks of rehearsal, the actor who was playing Jesse Kiplinger in the second act quit and I volunteered to play that role as well. Nick Philips played Roy Hubley in the third act. Muriel was played by an attractive young lady I had met a number of years earlier at a Theatre Newington function. The director, who was a doctor, had harbored some doubts about whether I could successfully carry off both roles and I will never forget his deep sighs of relief and satisfaction on opening night.

Ed Pizzella, as Buffalo Bill, with Desiree Saleski and Pat Keating.

"Annie Get Your Gun"—Ed Pizzella as Buffalo Bill.

"Annie Get Your Gun"—Tracey Barrone (Annie
Oakley) and Ed Pizzella (Buffalo Bill).

My next stage venture at Beckley was portraying the flamboyant Buffalo Bill in "Annie Get Your Gun." I got the biggest kick out of this role which allowed me to make use of my cowboy boots and .22 caliber pistols. I purchased a Stetson and then I went to the Salvation Army Store and picked up a leather coat. My mother sewed leather strips on the sleeves and I was in business.

I received a call from Terry, the drama teacher at the Avon Old Farms Boys' School. They were doing "Guys And Dolls" and had asked my ex-wife, Mel, to direct it. She was tied up and referred them to me. I met with Terry and we mapped out a schedule. I drove out there three afternoons a week for rehearsals. The girls from Miss Porter's School were bussed in to fill the female roles and the show played to an enthusiastic audience. The kids were fantastic and I thoroughly enjoyed the experience.

"Guys And Dolls" at Avon Old Farms Boys School—"Fugue For Tinhorns."

Kris McMurray was always interested in exploring new theatrical horizons. He had a long standing arrangement with a company that conducted bus tours under which KEM Productions would perform special shows on the road. These would usually be at hotels on evenings during the week or Sunday matinees. We'd get a couple of weeks' notice, do a couple of quick rehearsals, then load a pickup truck with props and set pieces and off we'd go.

In 1994, we did special performances of "Plaza Suite" at the Waterbury Sheraton and "Barefoot In The Park" at the Stamford Sheraton and at the Sheraton at Bradley International Airport. In 1995, we performed "Barefoot" at the Farmington Marriott.

Ed Pizzella and Joanne Callahan.

It was during these road trips that Kris made contact with the manager of the Bradley Sheraton and came up with the idea of doing Sunday matinees there. We put our heads together and named the enterprise "Broadway Brunch." There we did performances of "The Odd Couple," "Plaza Suite" and "Barefoot In The Park." I directed all three. Kris and I played Felix and Oscar in "The Odd Couple" and I recruited Joanne Callahan to share the stage with me in "Plaza Suite." I, of course, played Victor Velasco in "Barefoot."

"Breaking Legs." Ed Pizzella, as Lou Graziano.

The next production at Beckley was "Breaking Legs," a hilarious comedy in which a college professor, who is also a neophyte playwright, approaches his former student's father about financing the production of his play. His student works as a waitress in her father's Italian restaurant and she invites her professor to meet with her father and his friends to discuss the enterprise. Unbeknown to the professor, his student's father and friends are members of the Mafia. I directed and cast myself in the role of Lou Graziano, the restaurant owner, whose daughter is romantically involved with the professor. This was the role played by Vincent Gardenia on Broadway. Guy Camarca was cast in the role of Frankie Salvucci and Marty Kapper played Tino DeFelice.

"Breaking Legs." Lou Graziano and his associates toast the professor (left).

I enjoyed my involvement with this show because it gave me an opportunity to make use of my Italian heritage, but, at the same time, I was plagued by one of the most perturbing problems I had ever encountered. One of the cast members was extremely egotistical and openly insubordinate. It took all of the fortitude I could muster to keep from running him off the set, but, for the good of the show, I managed to keep my cool and the show was a hit.

The show was set in the restaurant and Kris cooked the delicious food that was served to us on stage by Angie. To add to the realism, during the show we played a tape of actual restaurant sounds coming from what was supposed to be the kitchen behind us.

The cast of "Love, Sex And The IRS."

"Love, Sex And The IRS"—Ed Pizzella (the tax man)
hits on Ginny Vilcinskas, Jon's girlfriend.

The next show at Beckley was a farce entitled "Love, Sex And The IRS," which was directed by Kris. I was cast as the IRS auditor and other members of the cast included Guy Camarca, who played the landlord, Ginny Vilcinskas, who played the girlfriend, and Gail Gregory, who played the mother.

The leading characters are Jon and Leslie, two young fellows who share an apartment in New York. Jon is an accountant and does their tax returns. Thinking that he can save them some money, he files joint returns indicating that Leslie is his wife. The scam works until they're audited and all hell breaks out. When the IRS man comes to investigate, Leslie dons a dress and wig and pretends to be Jon's wife. They get the tax man drunk and he chases Jon's girlfriend around the apartment.

The set for "Love, Sex And The IRS." Most of the set pieces were provided by Ed Pizzella and Ed made the "Le Club" sign.

I enjoyed playing a drunk again. It reminded me of my bit in "The Impossible Years." Every Time I chased Ginny, she'd hit me on the head with a break-away bottle. This expensive prop looked like the real thing, but was made of sugar and shattered like glass.

Dave Fitzgerald and I designed and constructed a number of window and door flats that could be connected and reassembled in different configurations to form a vast variety of sets. I provided the windows and flush paneled doors. I also designed and constructed the "LeClub" sign.

"The Sunshine Boys" at Beckley Gardens. Setting up for
the Doctor's skit. Chuck Rinaldi on the right.

I got a big kick out of directing "The Sunshine Boys" at
Beckley. I desperately wanted to cast myself in the role of
Willie Clark, but, at the time, I was also directing and acting
in a show for Broadway Brunch at the Bradley Sheraton and
it just would have been too much. I would have to wait until
2002 to do this role at the Connecticut Cabaret.

"The Sunshine Boys"—The Doctor's skit at Beckley Dinner Theatre.

Much of the humor in this show is bawdy and focuses on a sexy blond nurse. I searched high and low, but was unable to find an actress who would do justice to this role. At the time I was serving as the secretary for Newington Community Television, Inc. and, when I attended NCTV's monthly meeting, I met an attractive young woman named Sandy Miller. We struck up a conversation and I blurted out my predicament. Although she had no stage experience, she expressed an interest in filling the role and I invited her to attend the next rehearsal. She did and subsequently accepted the part. She performed admirably and little did I then know that several years later I would be dating her mother, Shirley.

Sandy Miller (the sexy Nurse) with Director, Ed Pizzella.

CHAPTER TWENTY-ONE

THE PRODIGAL'S RETURN

"Sugar Babies"—Julie Woloszczyk and Fred Desimini.

It was 1996 and Starlight had collapsed. Kris McMurray had talked about doing a replay of "Sugar Babies," but refused to give this idea any serious consideration without

Fred Desimini in the leading role. And the two were not talking. I contacted Fred, who was on a theatrical hiatus, and arranged for the two of them to meet. Miraculously they ironed out their differences and "Sugar Babies" was scheduled to go into production. Fred, of course, played the lead, supported by Joanne Callahan and Julie Woloszczyk. Al Barron was one of the comics and I again played the Candy Butcher and second comic.

"Sugar Babies"—(L-R) Christina Shortt and Fred Desimini, as Top Bannana.

"Sugar Babies"—Ed Pizzella as the Candy Butcher. Costume by Nonni.

I designed the set and Dave Fitzgerald and I built it. The backdrop consisted of a gleaming mylar-strip curtain behind a series of white arches bedecked with flashing white Christmas lights. Four swings were rigged so that they could be dropped and chorus girls could swing out into the audience.

"Sugar Babies"—(Top) Cast and crew. (Foreground) Joanne Callahan and Kris McMurray. (Background) Fred Desimini, Allison Beschler, Ed Pizzella, Dave Fitzgerald and Steve Ennis. (Below) Fred in the midst of the dancers.

"Sugar Babies"—Tracey Barone.

One of the members of the cast was Corky Mower. He was a part-time musician, who played in a small band. He invited the cast to one of his gigs. This was where I met his lovely, pregnant wife, Claudia. Corky and I became friends and he introduced me to his attractive, unattached mother-in-law, Shirley Miller. Shirley and I started dating and soon became a couple. I subsequently dubbed her Shu.

A Theatre Party. (L-R) Claudia and Corky Mower and Fred at right.

Then I was cast as Roscoe Clementine in a comedy entitled "A Little Quicky," which Kris directed at Beckley. The play was written by the same writers, who authored "Love, Sex And The IRS" and most of the cast members, who appeared in this show, had appeared in the prior comedy.

"A Little Quicky"—Ed Pizzella, as Roscoe Clementine, and Polly.

Kris's step-father, Jim Norman, operated a photo studio and took some wonderful publicity shots.

"A Little Quicky"—Roscoe and the girls.

One of Kris' favorite shows was "Nunsense." I built the lighted "Grease" sign and, because space on stage was limited, I designed and built a juke-box, which converted to a bed.

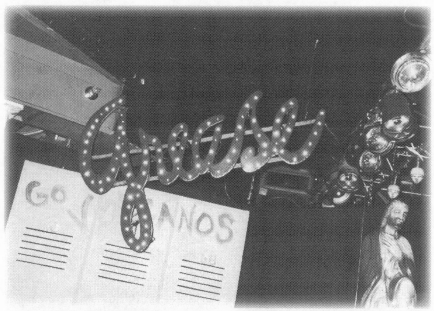

(Top) "Nunsense" at Beckley. The Grease sign. (Below) Ed
Pizzella, dressed as a priest, and Barbara Norman.

Since the show takes place at a Catholic school, I added
some local color by dressing as a priest and greeting the
audience.

"Nunsense" at Beckley. Melody Pizzella as Sister Robert Anne.

Kris later came up with the idea of doing the show in drag, but Samuel French, Inc., the company that held the right to license the show, refused to allow it to be staged in this manner and this kindled a feud with Jack Curtis, Beckley's owner. Curtis renewed his demands for a contract with a substantial penalty clause. Kris refused to enter into such a contract and Jack became so upset that he locked Kris out of the theatre and attempted to make a deal with the Castle Craig Players of Meriden to perform at Beckley. Kris moved his operation to Webster Square Road in Berlin and founded the Connecticut Cabaret.

(L-R) Kris McMurray, Melody Pizzella, Gail Gregory and Bobby DiCioccio.

Kris initiated a lawsuit against Curtis, but before the action could be concluded, Curtis went bankrupt and moved to Florida. The mortgage at Beckley was foreclosed and the property was subsequently sold and renovated.

CHAPTER TWENTY-TWO

HOME AT LAST

It was 1997 and, after his blowup with Jack Curtis, Kris McMurray moved his group to Webster Square Plaza in Berlin and established The Connecticut Cabaret Theatre. In 1999 he called me and told me he wanted to revive "Barefoot" and he asked me to take the role of Victor Velasco. In this version Julie Tremaglio played Corie. Kris, of course, was Paul Bratter and Gail Gregory was Mrs Banks.

"Barefoot In The Park" at the Connecticut Cabaret. Julie Tremaglio, as Corie Bratter and Ed Pizzella, as Victor Velasco.

"Barefoot In The Park"—Velasco on his way to the Four Winds.

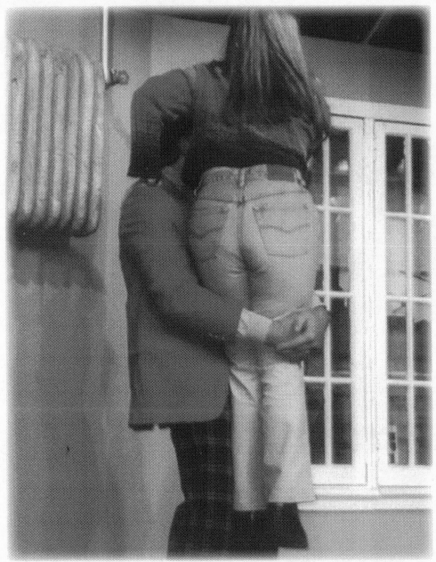

"Barefoot In The Park"—Velasco lifts Corie up to turn up the heat.

I really enjoyed the intimate atmosphere at the Cabaret and, although I missed Ginny, I was impressed with Julie's ability to effectively recreate the Corie Bratter, who the veteran members of the cast had come to know and love, since I first directed the show in 1985.

"Barefoot In The Park" at the Cabaret—(L-R) Kris McMurray, as Paul, Julie Tremaglio, as Corie, Ed Pizzella, as Velasco and Gail Gregory, as Mrs. Banks.

"Barefoot"—Velasco and Mrs. Banks. The next morning.

Bob Cumming, writing for Hometown News Publications, in the January 14, 2000 issue said that "Neil Simon's 'Barefoot In The Park,' the second of five productions [at the Connecticut Cabaret] between now and mid-June, is a titillating experience . . . CCT's splendid and secure cast brought to mind the 1967 movie version of 'Barefoot,' starring Robert Redford, Jane Fonda and Charles Boyer. Aiding the digestion of the many tables covered with BYO food . . . were laughs galore . . . . In the Charles Boyer role was a vibrant Ed Pizzella, to whom (along with Gail Gregory), McMurray dedicated the show. 'We have performed this show all over the entire state of Connecticut and it gives me great pleasure to finally bring it home to my theatre.'"

Corie and Mrs. Banks. Photo from Hometown News Publications-01/14/00.

(Top) Herald photo, 12/3199. (L-R) Ed Pizzella (Velasco), Gail Gregory (Mrs. Banks), Kris McMurray(Paul Bratter and Julie Tremaglio (Corie Bratter) . (Below) "Barefoot" at CCT—Corie, Paul and Velasco.

"Barefoot In The Park" at CCT—Velasco offers Mrs. Banks some knichi.

It was in this time frame that we were notified of the sudden and unexpected death of Al Barron of Southington, who had begun his theatrical career with Theatre One and with whom I was pleased to share the stage on so many memorable occasions. Al started his acting career with Theatre One and appeared in a number of shows I directed. I will never forget the naïveté he exhibited when he made his debut and I considered myself his theatrical mentor. We attended his memorial service, where I read a poetic eulogy I had written, entitled "If There's A Stage." It can be found in the appendix.

'Plaza Suite' playing
at Connecticut Cabaret
- Page 3

New Britain Herald photo. (Top) Edra Parker. (Below L-R)
Ed Pizzella, Joanne Callahan and Michael Gilbride.

My next show at the Cabaret was in 2001, when I played the role of Roy Hubley in the third act of "Plaza Suite." I enjoyed working again with Joanne Callahan, who played Mrs. Hubley. We had performed these roles two years earlier for Broadway Brunch at the Bradley Sheraton. It was a pleasure sharing the stage with Joanne because she was not only versatile and talented, but she was extremely vivacious, good humored and easy to work with.

"Plaza Suite" at the Connecticut Cabaret. (Standing) Ed Pizzella, as Roy Hubley in the Third Act. (Seated) Joanne Callahan, who appeared in all three acts, and Michael Gilbride, her husband in the First Act. (On the floor) Edra Parker, as Jesse Kiplinger in the Second Act.

"Plaza Suite" at the Cabaret. (L-R) Joanne Callahan (Mrs. Hubley), Matthew Marrero (the groom) and Ed Pizzella (Roy Hubley). Seated is Sandy Miller (Mimsey in the Third Act and the secretary in the First Act).

John Mastrandrea as the Rabbi in a comedy at the Conn. Cabaret.

In 2002, I teamed up with John Mastrandrea, a high school classmate of mine, to do another familiar Neil Simon classic at the Cabaret, "The Sunshine Boys." I, of course, played Willie Clark, John played Al Lewis, my estranged comedy partner, and George Lombardo played my attentive nephew and theatrical agent. John hadn't done any stage work in many years and when Kris McMurray was looking for an actor to play the part of a rabbi in a prior comedy, I called John and introduced him to the theatre. John is extremely energetic and blessed with a wonderful, wry sense of humor. The folks at the theatre absolutely adored him and when the opportunity to cast the two of us in a comedy presented itself, Kris jumped at it.

"The Sunshine Boys" at the Connecticut Cabaret. Ed Pizzella, as Willie Clark, and John Mastrandrea, as Al Lewis.

Working with John was a treat. It was like a long anticipated reunion. We would get together at his condominium in West Hartford to rehearse our lines and his lovely wife, Dixie, would be following the script. We used most

of the blocking that I had designed when I directed this show
at the Beckley Dinner Theatre in 1995.

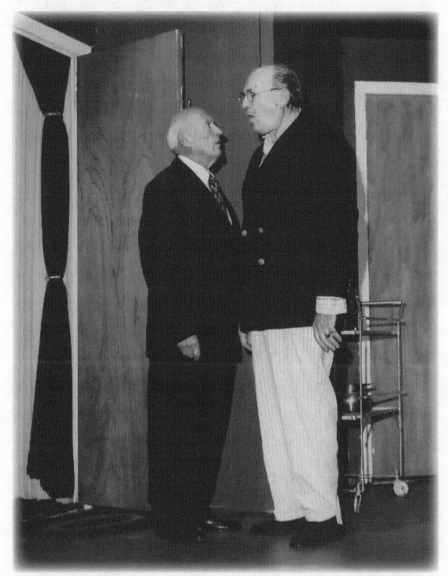

"The Sunshine Boys"—(L-R) John Mastrandrea (Al Lewis) and Ed Pizzella
(Willie Clark) confront each other after an eleven year separation.

I gave Willie an abrupt, sarcastic New York flavor and enjoyed
milking Neil Simon's hilarious lines. All three shows, "Barefoot,"
"Plaza Suite" and "The Sunshine Boys" played to packed houses.

"The Sunshine Boys"—(L-R) George Lombardo, the nephew, and Uncle Willie.

"The Sunshine Boys"—(Top) After eleven years, Willie talks to Al on the phone. (Below) Al and Willie prepare for the Doctor's skit on coast-to-coast television.

"The Sunshine Boys" at CCT—Willie's heart attack.

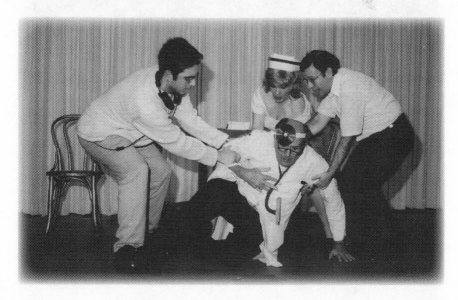

"The Sunshine Boys"—Willie recuperates with the help of his nurse and nephew.

"The Sunshine Boys" at CCT—United at last, Al and Willie have tea.

I was pleased with the vast variety of theatrical perspectives I had been exposed to in my lengthy stage career, which ironically began when, at the eleventh hour, I was induced to take a minor character role because an actor had abruptly walked out just before opening.

In "Count Dracula" I had played the same major role in three different theatres, working under different directors with diverging views of the script, performing twice in proscenium and once in three quarters. My experiences with "Little Shop Of Horrors" were similar, except that the disparities were compounded by my being called in to play the role at the very last moment on both occasions. In "The Odd Couple" I had played a leading role in different theatres working with different casts and crews, on the first occasion working under a new director and thereafter directing, as well as acting.

Likewise, in "The Last Of The Red Hot Lovers" I had performed the leading role in two different theatres working under different directors and with different casts and crews, but this was the most demanding of my many leading roles.

In "My Fair Lady" fate stepped in and I was cast at the eleventh hour to perform a leading role I had always longed to perform, when the actor originally cast walked out because he could not memorize the lines.

In "The Sound Of Music" I had played different roles in the same piece in different theatres, working under different directors, while in "Barefoot In The Park" I had directed and played the same major role in a dozen different theatre settings working with a variety of casts and crews. Of all of the shows I have done, "Barefoot" is the one I have performed on the greatest number of occasions and in the greatest variety of circumstances. Kris, Gail and I were able to put this show together virtually on 24-hours' notice.

In "Guys & Dolls" and "The Best Little Whorehouse In Texas" I had performed the same leading role in different theatres, on some occasions with the same director, cast and crew, and on others with different directors, casts and crews.

And finally in "Plaza Suite" and "The Sunshine Boys" I had experienced the thrill of directing and playing major roles in the same piece, but in different theatre settings with different casts and crews, sometimes just acting, sometimes just directing and sometimes doing both simultaneously.

Motivated by a host of brilliant and perceptive playwrights, I had mounted a mystical magic carpet and, transcending the limitations of time and space, stepped into the shoes of:

- a comical Irish tax collector, duped by the antics of three beer-befuddled matrons in a San Diego junkyard;
- a proud and successful middle-aged entrepreneur, humbled and confused by the alarming discovery that he is soon to become the father of a change-of-life baby;
- a crude and slovenly, chauvinistic, sports writer, driven to distraction by his roommate, an effeminate, male, hypochondriac neatnik;
- a know-it-all author-psychiatrist, who holds himself out to be an expert in dealing with teenagers and is exposed as a fraud by his two teenaged daughters;
- the founding fathers of a small New England town;

- the radical, self-confidant editor of a protest magazine, whose left-wing principles are compromised when he falls in love with a conservative Southern girl;
- an affable Irish cop entangled in a love triangle;
- a bumbling American ambassador stuck behind the iron curtain during the Cold War;
- a middle-aged husband, who, while reluctantly accompanying his wife shopping for twin beds, shares a mattress with an attractive salesgirl and tries to make a date with her;
- a senile, octogenarian birdwatcher, engaged with his spouse in a conversation of hilarious circuitous gibberish;
- a prestigious bank president whose job is endangered when his teenaged daughter tries out for the football team;
- a brutally honest theatre critic, who mercilessly pans his wife's performance;
- a psychotic, middle-aged corporate executive traumatized by depression when, after many years, he becomes the victim of corporate down-sizing;
- a romantic presidential candidate, who sings his way to the White House on a platform of universal love;
- a childishly enthusiastic, but sometimes frustrated, vampire-slaying Dutch professor;
- the terrified treasurer of a robot manufacturer, who rushes to his death in the midst of an attack by an angry mob composed of the company's products, who have joined to annihilate mankind;
- an elite society gentleman, who frequents a seedy bar on the docks of San Francisco;
- a down-to-earth Irish longshoreman;
- a devoutly principled, illegal Italian immigrant, who, to save his honor, fights and kills his American benefactor;
- a romantic, Pacific Island plantation owner, who, during World War II, falls in love with an American navy nurse;
- an English Lord caught in a family feud;
- a priest, who consoles the family of a hopelessly deluded and obsessive, senile uncle and seeks

to curtail his erratic escapades, which are gullibly intended to right all wrongs;

- a psychiatrist pitted against an imaginary six-foot rabbit;
- a benevolent millionaire, who befriends an orphan girl and her dog;
- a Russian General, who is mortified when he inadvertently sneezes on his superior;
- a Russian father, who introduces his sexually inexperienced son to a prostitute;
- a New York gambler, who hosts a floating crap game and continually seeks to elude the grasp of his loving, but addle-brained fiancée, intent upon marital conquest;
- the confidant to an incorrigible female bon vivant, who, as guardian of her nephew, instructs him in the relentless pursuit of life's pleasures;
- a respected lawman, who, because of the incessant, self righteous, moral rantings of an egotistical, publicity-hungry crusader, is traumatized when he is ordered to close down his girlfriend's brothel;
- a naval captain who risks his life and the lives of his family, when he leads them in their escape from the clutches of the Nazis;
- a warrior king who battles with his pacifist son;
- a fire and brimstone southern preacher;
- the wealthy sibling of an unemployed and depressed, middle-aged corporate executive, who reluctantly lends his brother the money to satisfy a lifelong fantasy;
- a middle-aged husband and restaurant owner who, in the throes of a mid-life crises, naively and unsuccessfully experiments with three extra-marital affairs;
- a zany, Bohemian, New York attic dweller, who courts the reserved mother of a newly-wed neighbor;
- the unpredictable, schizophrenic, but mellifluous announcer and emcee of a live audience radio variety show that takes place in December, 1942;
- the cantankerous, loud-mouthed owner of the Washington Senators;
- the whimsical wizard in a musical fantasy;

- a father, who deceptively conspires with his next door neighbor to induce his daughter to fall in love with the boy next door;
- the biblical father of a dozen sons, who, by making the most gifted of them his pet, induces the others to become jealous and to sell him into slavery;
- the Yiddish owner of a flower shop, who is devoured by a man-eating plant grown in his shop by his adoptive son;
- a wealthy bachelor who hires a matchmaker to find him a bride and ends up marrying the matchmaker;
- the respectable and unimpeachable mayor of a small town, which has succumbed to the irresistible charms and chicanery of an itinerant huckster;
- a pompous English dialectician who wagers that he can transform a cockney guttersnipe into a high bred society lady;
- an Argentine dictator who falls in love with and is manipulated by an attractive, domineering and ambitious trollop;
- a flamboyant and parasitical theatrical agent, who unsuccessfully tries to create a love-match between his friends, an attractive and arrogant Baroness and a serious, ethical and unwavering naval captain, who is the widowed and devoted father of seven children;
- an unfaithful, middle-aged husband who is forced to confess his infidelity to his dowdy wife on their wedding anniversary;
- a wily, egotistical, duplicitous Hollywood film producer who, on a trip to the east coast, salaciously seduces a former girlfriend;
- the impatient, irate, frustrated and confused father of a bride-to-be, who, on her wedding day, desperately tries to get her out of the hotel bathroom in which she has deliberately locked herself;
- the father of a precocious, talented and expressive young boy, who is destined to become one of America's foremost playwrights;
- a middle-aged, widowed butcher who meets with the father of a young girl to bargain for her hand

in marriage, while the father labors under the misapprehension that the butcher wants to buy his cow;

- the agile, outspoken and provocative leader of a band of elderly fur thieves;
- a world renowned buffalo hunter, who forms and successfully tours with a wild west show; and finally
- an Italian restaurant owner with Mafia connections, whose daughter falls in love with her English professor and tries to impress him by arranging for him to meet with her father and his unsavory friends in order to convince them to finance the production of a play the professor has written.

Little did I know then, as a naïve eighth-grade student in Miss Hoye's English class at Northeast Junior High School, when I bravely stood before my classmates and enthusiastically recited those poignant words of John Gillespie Magee, Jr., that I, in my lifetime, would actually experience the rapture so eloquently expressed by his inspirational poem, "High Flight:"

"Oh! I have slipped the surly bonds of Earth
And danced the skies on laughter-silvered wings.
Sunward I've climbed and joined the tumbling mirth
Of sun-split clouds—and done a hundred things
You have not dreamed of—wheeled and soared and swung
High in the sunlit silence. Hov'ring there,
I've chased the shouting wind along and flung
My eager craft through footless halls of air.
Up, up the long, delirious burning blue
I've topped the wind-swept heights with easy grace,
Where never lark, or even eagle flew.
And, with silent, lifting mind, I've trod
The high untrespassed sanctity of space,
Put out my hand and touched the face of God."

All of this, of course, could not have been possible without the inspiration and motivation abundantly provided by my intimate exposure to the infinite versatility of chairs.

APPENDIX

THE CRITIC

A reviewer's as sour as apples picked green,
For thought he's enjoyed a show that he's seen,
He'd never admit the actors were good
For fear that his comments might be understood.

Nor would he praise the style of direction,
For every endeavor requires correction.
And what about costumes, props, sets and dance?
He'd never concede that the show they enhance.

The web that he spins must be veiled in mystique,
The ire of his readers to cleverly pique.
Kudos and raves would never suffice
To artfully showcase this pundit's advice.

With candor he boasts of the knowledge he hoards.
To hell with the guys who ply on the boards!
They're just the kids this parent must scold.
Though lacking their talent, he's pompous and bold.

He gleefully points to the flaws he decries,
Proclaiming to all he's theatrically wise.
He often ignores the merits and pluses
To highlight the flubs, which at length he discusses.

And when he's completed his lethal incision,
He expects all his readers to reach one decision;
Not about theatre, to laud or to blame,
But just that this "critic" has earned his good name.

IF THERE'S A STAGE

[Dedicated to the fond memory of
Harry "Al" Barron of Southington]

Who is this man I felt I knew?
What made him dear to me?
This type of person's all too few,
Which now is clear to me.

He loved his family, one and all.
To him their place was number one.
But next he loved a curtain call.
Performing was his fun.

A dozen years ago we met,
Auditioning for a show.
He had a vim I'll not forget,
A radiant theatre glow.

A wide-eyed cherub filled with awe
Surrendered to his yearning.
He noted all he heard and saw,
Eager to be learning.

In "Radio Hour" he played old Pops.
His Applegate was quite a treat.
He coyly pulled out all the stops,
As Kipplinger in "Plaza Suite."

He thus began his stage career
Disclosing great ability,
But we who knew him had no fear
That he'd lose his humility.

In "Dracula" the English Doc;
In "My Fair Lady," Pickering;
His Melvin Thorpe fit like a sock.
Adeptly did he sing.

In "Sugar Babies" he was drole,
Though sometimes backstage he might doze.
Every time he took a role
A new character arose.

He loved to make an audience laugh.
He loved to hear applause.
He earned respect from crew and staff.
Perfection was his cause.

He was a pleasure to direct,
Because he truly loved his art,
Which he sought always to perfect,
Though large or small the part.

We worked together as a team
In "Opal" and in "Outward Bound."
The hours spent like minutes seem
And the time devoted would astound.

"The Odd Couple," our pride and joy,
Was several times repeated.
Complaining of the smoke was Roy,
Who claimed that Oscar cheated.

I felt secure with him on stage.
I knew he always had his line.
We memorized page after page
And he had faith that I had mine.

Of each achievement he was proud.
His family came to each event.
His gait was sure; his voice was loud
And he relished every moment spent.

Theatre quenched his avid thirst
And on the stage he had few peers.
His crowning jewel was "Who's On First,"
A joy we shared for years.

Through every trial he kept his cool.
He learned the rules and lived them well.
Though on the stage he played the fool,
In life and art did he excel.

This chapter's written, so turn the page.
We'll surely miss him, we who care,
But if in heaven there's a stage,
You can bet that he'll be there.

A KNIGHT TO REMEMBER

[Based on the musical play "Man Of LaMancha"]

The greatest story ever told is not what you might think,
But the story of a man, whose mind teetered on the brink.
In bygone days, it's said he roamed LaMancha's barren plain
And his larks, though well intentioned, brought him much disdain.

He'd read vivid tales of chivalry and legends of brave knights
And on their gallant escapades he staunchly set his sights.
Though withered by his many years, he would not be dismayed,
As he donned his makeshift armor and embarked on his crusade.

He vowed to seek out every wrong and every wrong he'd right,
So on his noble steed rode off this avid would-be knight.
Soon he stopped a barber and his shaving basin stole,
Which served him as a helmet in playing out his role.

Encountering a flock of sheep, he went into a trance
And, thinking them an evil hoard, attacked with sword and lance.
For this the shepherds beat him, fighting fire with fire,
And left him in a crumpled heap attended by his squire.

He next attacked a windmill, which seemed an evil giant,
And was brutally repelled in a manner quite defiant.
Weary of their battles, an inn they chanced to see,
Which to this tattered, would-be knight meant hospitality.

Here he might be dubbed, as was done in the days of old,
So to prepare his wilted spirit, a "vigil" he would hold.
He was led into a courtyard, where he fell upon his knee,
And there was boldly tempted by pompous vanity.

Humbled and ashamed, he confessed and bowed his head.
"Call nothing thine, except thy soul," remorsefully he said
And, fearing that to pride he might reluctantly succumb,
"Love not thy present self, but what thou may become."

There he met Aldonza with manner crude and base
And saw his Dulcinea, an angel, in her place.
Through his faith unwavering, she finally became
A lady of high character befitting that fair name.

Many are the follies that this befuddled knight befell,
Which are skillfully recounted by his author, Don Miguel.
He's frequently described as mad, for reason he defies,
"But, when life itself seems lunatic, who knows where madness lies?

Perhaps to be too practical is madness of a kind,
Or seeking wealth and treasure, where trash is left behind.
To give up dreams may be as mad as too much sanity,
Or seeing life as it is and not as it should be."

The saga of this hapless knight, by which I'm deeply stirred,
Is both profound and bittersweet and yet sometimes absurd.
Some think of Don Quixote as an old and senile clod,
Forgetting that the madman is called "a child of God."

Such are the timeless lessons that this madman's life portrayed.
Would that such a role might by all of us be played.

THE MODEL WIFE

Mounting disdain for the likes of womankind
Lured him to a bogus world of dreams,
Where ugly human flaws are difficult to find
And imagined virtue ever brightly gleams.

He fortified creative mind and will,
This sculptor of myth whom all admire,
And fashioned with patience, care and skill
The object of his own true love's desire.

A femme fatale in every fine detail,
Each feature a perfect work of art,
Though lifeless with complexion wan and pale,
He fondled her and offered her his heart.

Not in wildest fantasy dared he contemplate
That this inert female form would come to life,
Nor that this ivory model of what appeared an ideal mate
Would someday turn to flesh and be his wife.

Boundless were caresses he'd lovingly bestow
With ample gifts of flowers, birds and beads.
Silken garments for seductive limbs artfully he'd sew
With an ardor which from depth of love proceeds.

Rings upon her fingers and earrings in her ears,
And strings of pearls he'd place upon her breast.
He'd gaze upon her body with happiness and tears,
And on puffs of softest down lay her to rest.

It happened that the festival of Venus was at hand
And there our melancholy sculptor went to pray:
"O Goddess of Love, only you can understand
The bitter-sweet emotions to which I'm sadly prey.

Behold a tired artisan whose ember's lost its glow,
Whose artistic motivation withers in his soul.
I need a loving woman who'll go where'er I go,
Who, when I grieve, my spirit will console."

He petitioned for a spouse that he could call his own
In the semblance of the model he'd designed.
Venus knew at once, on the basis of his tone,
That metamorphosis is what he had in mind.

On the altar, as an omen, flames suddenly arose
To say that by the goddess he'd been heard.
He returned to find his statue in her customary pose
With no clue a transformation had occurred.

Lips that once were cold, now were moist and warm.
He saw in her a glow he'd never seen.
Rigidity no longer was her sedentary norm,
For a truly vibrant woman had replaced his figurine.

Here a basic truth can readily be learned,
Which no objective mind would dare deny.
Beauty is a gift which with labor must be earned,
And a goal which to embrace we all must try.

As with the maid that brought Pygmalion fame,
The artist to beauty is inescapably betrothed,
And for expression of his love he strives with pain,
Until her essence in artistic form's exposed.

The bottom line is to every artist clear;
Love repressed within his soul does through his art appear.

THE PRINCE OF DREAMS

(Based upon the Book of Genesis, Chap. 35 et seq.)

God appeared to Jacob, whom he named Israel,
And in the land of Canaan decreed that he should dwell.
"Multiply!" was his command,
"And build ye nations on the land,"
Which heavenly directives pious Jacob heeded well.

Responding to the edicts, which from the Lord he got,
Jacob, now called Israel, a dozen sons begot.
The product of four mothers,
Contentious were these brothers,
Whose fraternal interaction forms the basis of our plot.

Unequivocally was Joseph the favorite of his dad,
Which was bound to foster jealousy and make his siblings mad.
They were Ruben, Levi, Simian,
Juda, Dan and Benjamin,
Nephtali, Aser, Zabulon, Issachar and Gad.

Young Joseph was endowed with a power that was rare,
A talent to which no other could possibly compare.
Adept at analyzing dreams,
He would prophesy, it seems,
And in numerous predictions never err.

This wizard to his brothers one day a dream revealed.
"While harvesting the stalks that had ripened in the field.
To those I held, yours humbly bowed,"
Which garnered protests long and loud
And so incensed his siblings that the braggart's fate was sealed.

Ignoring animosity beneath his very nose,
He did to this disgruntled group another dream disclose.
"I saw myself as moon and sun,
While eleven stars around me spun,"
An image which propelled them to the verge of casting blows.

Though surely it was not at all intended by their sire,
Consistently did Jacob pour fuel upon the fire
By his fawning over Joe,
Knowing not that he would sow
Latent seeds of envy that would blossom into ire.

Making matters worse, Joe was clearly Jacob's pet
And his feelings for this child he'd not allow them to forget.
To show paternal pride,
He kept Joseph by his side,
Expressing deep concern whene'er the youth might fret.

To the apple of his eye, his father made a gift,
Thinking Joseph's dampened spirits he might thereby lift;
'Twas a coat of many hues
Designed to dissipate the blues,
But in the end it only served to broaden sibling rift.

These incidents occurred in the days when life was crude
And a shepherd found it difficult providing for his brood.
With discipline in mind,
Chores were liberally assigned
That each might learn the value of his shelter and his food.

Thus this multitude of issue, whom did lusty Jacob spawn,
Assisted him in tending sheep each day from crack of dawn.
In the wilderness they'd roam
And vowed, when one day they got home,
That he whom they despised would soon be gone.

They'd whisper to each other each time they got a chance
The removal of this nuisance to ultimately advance.
"Exhausting all our bonafides,
This guy's a thorn in all our sides,
So let's rid ourselves of 'Mr. Fancy-pants.'"

Jealousy and envy can heated words inspire,
Expressing not at all what the speakers may desire.
When the pressure is increased,
It must somehow be released
And may cause the desperate victims to conspire.

"Murder is the answer," the conspirators agreed,
"And from his egocentric boasting we'll at last be freed.
We'll drop him bloody in a pit
And finally we'll be rid of it,
And with contrivance and mendacity we'll cover up the deed.

His ostentatious coat we'll gladly take and shred,
Announcing with despair that we found it on him dead.
The victim of a roving beast
Will be our brother, now deceased,
Whom we will mourn with ample tears and lowered head."

But Ruben for his brother retained an ounce of care
And thus convinced the others that his life they ought to spare.
So this very angry crew
From fratricide withdrew
And decided that instead they would simply leave him there.

Thus headlong in the pit was the boastful dreamer cast,
Though they knew that without water he'd not last.
Then Juda voiced a comment bold,
Suggesting that the boy be sold
To a wandering band of Ishmaelites, who then were strolling past.

To the country known as Egypt were these gypsy merchants bound
To peddle myrrh and frankincense and spices by the pound.
In that land of many knaves
Jews were bought and sold as slaves
And markets for such human wares did everywhere abound.

To purchase the outcast they the nomads did entice
And twenty silver pieces was bargained as the price.
Thus the boy they never slew,
But from that nasty pit withdrew
And off was he to Egypt to be sold as merchandise.

The motley, ragged shreds of the loathsome prophet's coat
Were splattered with the blood of a newly slaughtered goat.
They to Jacob then were given,
As proof that Joseph wasn't livin',
And in the tears his father shed a ship, no doubt, could float.

When in Egypt they arrived, for ages it's been told,
To Potiphar, the Captain, the youthful Jew was sold
To be a servant in his house
At the beck and call of spouse,
Who did the handsome lad with loving eyes behold.

Unbeknown to her husband, with lust his wife did burn,
As she pursued the bashful youth with zeal at every turn.
When he rejected her advance,
She tore swatches from his pants
And taught posterity a lesson that every male should learn.

To her unsuspecting husband, she gave the pieces torn.
"The servant-boy seduced me!" she stubbornly had sworn.
When his defense completely failed,
Joe was quickly chained and jailed,
Proving hell hath not the fury to match a woman's scorn.

This confirms a frightening fact we conveniently forget,
That Man is plagued with flaws, which have origins long set,
And to this very day
With clarity display
The need for introspection, repentance and regret.

Now to add a novel twist to our loosely woven tale,
Pharaoh's disreputed butler and his baker were in jail.
Each was haunted by a dream,
Knowing not what it might mean,
And on Joseph's intuition did officiously prevail.

The butler disclosed that in his dream he'd seen a vine
With three fruit-laden branches, ideal for making wine.
He squeezed the grapes in Pharaoh's cup
And, when the King had drunk it up,
He found the taste to be both exotic and divine.

"The triple branches," Joseph said, "signify three days,
After which your loyal service His Majesty will praise.
Your office he'll restore,
As it had been before,
And you'll return again to serve in many fruitful ways."

He exacted from the butler, when he should be restored,
His promise that he'd speak Joseph's praises to his Lord,
That he might then be freed
And the butler quite agreed,
For 'twas the only form of recompense such prisoners could afford.

When the optimistic baker all these hopeful things had heard,
He approached the noted prophet and sought to have a word
And this is what he said:
"I dreamed that balanced on my head
Were three baskets filled with meat, which were eaten by a bird."

Intently Joseph pondered the meaning of the dream,
Knowing that its impact would on the baker be extreme.
With remorse and deep dismay,
He found it difficult to say
That the baker's days were numbered, it would seem.

"Your remaining days of life are sadly naught but three,
After which, I'm pained to say, your execution's what I see.
Since you've betrayed your boss,
He will hang you on a cross,"
He reluctantly foretold with utmost sympathy.

The prophecies, as spoken, in due course were fulfilled,
With which the butler, now restored, undoubtedly was thrilled,
But his promise he forgot,
For he spoke of Joseph not
And in prophetic benefactor sharp bitterness instilled.

From these events a year elapsed and then another year,
And it came to pass that nightmares caused His Majesty to fear.
The king recalled that in his dream
He was standing by a stream,
From which seven healthy cows seemed strangely to appear.

As in leisure these were grazing contently on the shore,
From this brook of mystery there came forth seven more.
The latter, being sick and lean,
Devoured those whom first he'd seen,
But yet remained as scrawny, as they appeared before.

The second dream concerned some luscious ears of corn.
Seven, full and fair, on a single stalk were borne.
There then grew seven more,
Sickly, thin and sore,
And ate the first, which from the stalk savagely were torn.

Gathering all his counselors from distant shores and near,
The King described his dreams and his consequential fear.
None the meaning could present,
Or even guess at what was meant
And it was then that the memory of the butler became clear.

He recalled the events, which in prison had occurred;
How from Joseph the meaning of his reverie he'd heard;
That though the prophet was a Jew,
All the things he said came true
And he delighted in recalling every single word.

Pharaoh, by what he'd heard, was instantly inspired
And no longer could rely on the counselors he had hired.
He could dally not a jot,
But must know his future lot
And thus to meet the sorcerer he fervently desired.

Thence was Joseph quickly summoned to the throne,
Where the King to him his dreams made fully known.
"These," said Joe, "are really one
And tell us now what must be done.
God has spoken to you, Sire, as to his very own.

Healthy cattle are the same as healthy ears,
Which means abundant will be crops for seven years,
And what will follow, have no doubt,
Will be seven years of drought,
For which we must prepare, or else shed ample tears."

The prediction he repeated, so all should understand,
That at first there'd be abundance in the land,
Which would be followed by starvation,
Affecting those of every nation,
But with foresight a solution could be planned.

Massive barns for storage he proposed that they should build
And with a fifth part of each harvest should annually be filled.
"During every year of plenty,
Fill them up; leave no part empty!"
And when these words the monarch heard, this is what he willed.

The prophet then proposed, before it was too late,
That the office of Director the sovereign should create,
Who would travel through the nation
And provide an explanation,
That with this plan the citizens might then cooperate.

What happened next was something quite bizarre,
For though the prisoner was a stranger from afar,
The King with him agreed
And Joseph quickly freed,
Appointing him the magistrate, which made of him a czar.

By the silver tongue of Joseph was Pharaoh truly swayed
And from the path the Jew laid out the monarch never strayed.
Though by some was Joe attacked,
By his record he was backed,
So the King faced the adventure unafraid.

The sovereign then in gratitude announced throughout the land
That Joseph was to be his second in command.
Giving thanks for what was told,
Pharaoh showered him with gold,
Presenting him a ring, which he took from his own hand.

This handsome Jew, whose words were wise and sage,
Had made indelible his mark on history's page.
His talent vastly changed his life
And now the King gave him a wife,
When he had reached but thirty years of age.

As though he'd seen a vision within a crystal ball,
The events that he foretold did accordingly befall
And safe from devastation
Was this solitary nation,
For catastrophic famine struck the others, one and all.

To Egypt all her neighbors came for grain
And Joseph sold the surplus they needed not retain.
Canaan suffered like the others,
From whence came Joseph's brothers,
For not a stitch of food did their cupboards then contain.

Benjamin, the youngest, with his father stayed behind,
Fearing all the rigors and the perils they might find.
Direct to Joseph came the ten,
Unaware that he was one of them,
But Joe recognized his brothers and to heckle them inclined.

Not having seen their sibling, since he was very young,
They knew him not in royal robe, nor knew his foreign tongue.
Nor did they have a clue
This man could be a Jew,
For in this land no Canaanite could reach so high a rung.

Joseph longed to play a game with his unsuspecting kin,
As from the outset he absolved them from their youthful sin.
He enjoyed each moment spent,
Seeing they were innocent,
And with a mischievous charade did he begin.

"You are spies," he declared with robust anger feigned,
While with laughter in his bosom he was pained.
They begged and vainly pleaded
That it was only food they needed
And cowered at the thought that ironic vengeance reigned.

With feelings of contempt that could not be controlled,
Years ago in bondage had they their brother sold.
To Egypt was he taken,
Where now, ironically forsaken,
Were they oppressed by strangers, whose attitudes were cold.

Their father, they confessed, was at home with youngest brother
And insisted that their goal was simply food and no other.
Their pleading was to no avail,
For Joseph threw them all in jail,
While the joy he held inside he found difficult to smother.

For three long days in prison were they in jest confined
And pained were they by guilt that weighed heavy on their mind
About the brother they'd abused,
Who was, unbeknown to them, amused,
As contritely they recalled how to him they'd been unkind.

From jail were they released and Joseph gathered them around.
"Bring me Benjamin," he said, "when at home he may be found."
He filled their sacks with grain
And sent them home again,
Making Simian his hostage, whom he ordered to be bound.

Compensation for their food they gladly paid,
Unaware of the arrangements Joe had made,
For within each bulging sack,
When the brothers turned their back,
His servants hid their money that the price might be repaid.

On their homeward journey, when their sacks they did unbind,
The money they had paid they then and there did find.
Thanking God for this event,
For all their savings had been spent,
The mysterious repayment of their money eased their mind.

When at home, safe and sound, they arrived,
They were grateful the ordeal had been survived.
Although extremely tired,
They recounted what transpired
And then wondered if the refund was contrived.

Angered was Jacob by what he had been told
And proceeded his nine sons to sharply scold.
"Joseph by a beast was felled
And Simian's by Pharaoh held
And now he seeks our youngest to behold?

What is it now that you would ask of me?
The sons I will have lost will number three!"
But savvy Ruben swore,
"I'll see you lose no more!
Benjamin will be my charge. I'll bring him back, you'll see!"

Juda, quite embarrassed, did explanation make,
"Benjamin, our brother, was mentioned by mistake.
We were caught by surprise
And must bring him, otherwise
In the future no food will we authorized to take.

Pharaoh's governor accused us all of spying
And, as evidence that we had not been lying,
Ordered Benjamin be brought
Before any food be bought,
Which is why we gave our oath," he ended, sighing.

When the food that they had purchased was depleted,
It was vital that the journey be repeated.
Jacob sent them back for more
On condition they restore
The son whom to the foreigners they'd ceded.

Many splendid gifts for the Pharaoh they prepared
In the hope that their brothers would in the end be spared.
Double money did they take
To correct the past "mistake"
And to prove their family honor unimpaired.

When to Joseph in their need they had returned,
Bringing Benjamin with whom he was concerned,
A feast he ordered to be spread,
Which all attended, breaking bread,
But in the brothers' guilty minds suspicions churned.

They thought they might be victims of a plot
Concerning the repayment they had got
And told the steward they had more,
With which to even up the score,
But he hastened to explain they owed him not.

When Joseph saw young Benjamin, he cried
And, weeping, left the room to save his pride.
Still they knew him not,
Or why emotional he got
And his identity continued he clandestinely to hide.

When their stomachs and their sacks again were filled
And they had paid whatever price they had been billed,
Brother Simian was freed
And, with everything they'd need,
Homeward bound were they again, as Jacob willed.

To play another joke on his brothers Joseph tried
And in his servants did he secretly confide.
He told them to restore
All their money, as before,
And in the bag of brother, Benjamin, a golden cup to hide.

When the entourage had reached the city gate,
They were stopped by palace guards, who there did wait.
Asked if they'd committed theft,
When the palace they had left,
In unison their innocence they emphatically did state.

A search of their possessions was protested loud and strong,
As they vehemently swore that they had done no wrong.
The guards with eldest did begin
And in the sack of Benjamin
Was found the royal chalice, which there did not belong.

To the palace they were forcibly returned,
Confused and with their future much concerned.
"At home we should have stayed,
For our father we've betrayed!
'Tis a lesson we should long ago have learned!"

When escorted to Joseph, whom sheepishly they hailed,
He announced with indignation that their youngest must be jailed.
All were very sad,
Feeling they'd let down their dad,
And pleaded for his freedom, but in the effort failed.

About their own well-being, concerned not in the least,
They demanded that their brother be released.
Each proposed to take his place
And punishment agreed to face
That the anguish of their father be decreased.

When Joseph did such genuine and selfless love behold,
His emotions could no longer be controlled.
That they were brothers he confessed
And his love for them professed
And he showered them with gifts of wealth untold.

Then did he explain the cards that had been dealt
And pleased was he to say how happy he now felt.
Telling of each playful jest,
He said that they had passed the test,
For the love his brothers shared caused all bitterness to melt.

"No woeful pangs of guilt should your heavy hearts contain,
For the mishaps of yester year did heaven preordain.
What in your youth you did to me
Were things that simply had to be,
So that later I could save you all from pain."

The memories of his youth he feared in time might fade,
So the coat of many colors he caused to be remade.
Eyes were dazzled by its hues,
Its reds and greens and poignant blues,
As the garment, so unique, he flamboyantly displayed.

With pride he donned the coat, which to his eyes brought tears,
For he recalled that in his youth it had so inflamed his peers.
He had dreamed of this event,
That here his family would be sent,
So that he could give them comfort in their remaining years.

He absolved them from their youthful acts of sin
And beseeched them to bring Jacob and their kin.
In Egypt they would make their home,
Never more to fear or roam,
A new abundant life there to begin.

From this story one may basic lessons glean.
To one's neighbor one should not be cruel or mean.
Be thou ready to forgive.
'Tis the way we all should live,
As from the outcome of this legend can be seen.

To the word of God open up your ear
And, in performance of His edicts, have no fear.
Never give up hope,
Learn with obstacles to cope
And always hold your family members dear.

Be not fearful that your goals you'll not attain,
Because of heritage, or race, or family name.
If you're more than just a fop,
Be assured you'll reach the top,
If self-esteem and perseverance you sustain.

TRAGIC RENDEZVOUS

Pyramus and Thisbe were parted by a wall,
Whose rugged stones obstructed love's caress.
And neither had an inkling of events that would befall
In their vain and tragic search for happiness.

Their plight was by observers dimly viewed
And proximity did not their fate enhance,
For their families were embittered by a feud,
Which offered little hope for their romance.

No contact was allowed between the two,
So in stealth did Thisbe whisper in a crack.
The devotion of her lover well she knew,
When surreptitious vows he whispered back.

So intense was their affection that each touch upon the stone
Sent detectable vibrations that reached the other side.
Thus despite their separation, neither party felt alone,
But they found themselves adrift upon a tide.

On a secret rendezvous did they finally agree,
For passion had induced them to conspire.
So, in the dark of night beneath a certain tree
At last would they attain their heart's desire.

She was first to reach the designated spot
And patiently she waited in the stillness of the night.
Frustration was destined to be the maiden's lot,
For a lioness appeared and Thisbe fled in mortal fright.

In her hurry to escape, frantic Thisbe dropped her shawl,
As to a hollow crag in frenetic haste she went.
She knew not that the savage beast the garment lost would maul,
For laden was the fabric with her scent.

Predator and frightened maid this place had long departed,
When tardy Pyramus beneath the tree arrived.
Discovery of the bloody scarf made him heavy hearted,
For he thought she'd been attacked and not survived.

Feeling guilt for her demise, he ended life's routine,
For he lacked the will to live without her charms.
At this very moment Thisbe entered on the scene
To hold her dying lover in her arms.

The tattered shawl explained why he had forfeited his life
And bitterly she wept o'er his demise.
Deeply in her bosom she plunged
his bloody knife
And, whispering words of love, she closed her eyes.

The massive tree with berries pearly white,
Wept for the lovers, who lay dying 'neath its spread
And the splatters of their blood, like a raging blight,
Turned its grieving, pallid fruit to ruby red.

The Mulberry thus stands from other trees apart,
As the tombstone of lovers death was powerless to part.

VITAL VITTLES

"What's the food of life," you ask?
"What nurtures us for life's travails?
Can it be found in box or flask,
Or canisters or pails?"

Life's a banquet, I assure you,
Replete with every tempting dish.
Candied hopes and smiles will lure you.
What need is there for meat or fish?

Before each hungry soul it's spread.
You'd think that folks would die to taste it.
But few are those whom it has fed.
On multitudes it's wasted.

This fabled feast to all exposes
Delicious treats that satiate,
Seducing eyes and tongues and noses,
And causing guests to salivate.

A potpourri of promises,
Their prompt fulfillment realized;
Quiches crammed with hugs and kisses;
Fidelity that's caramelized;

Naughty notions by the scoop;
Ambitions lightly toasted;
Ripe reflections stirred in soup;
Inventive genius roasted;

A salad of nostalgic greens;
Puddings spiced with precious time;
Bowls of bright bucolic scenes;
Tarts of lilting song and rhyme;

Omelets drenched with melted dreams;
Entertainments diced and grilled;
Pastas tossed with saucy themes,
And crepes with inspirations filled;

A thick fondue of reveries;
Cuddles wrapped within a bun;
Steaming pots of pleasantries;
Tangy fricassees of fun;

Hors d'oeuvres of crisp, creative thought;
Aspirations flaked and browned;
Infectious humor freshly caught,
Baked in fritters, plump and round;

A smorgasbord of flattery
With gentle denigrations;
Canapés of empathy
With drizzled expectations;

Nestled in exotic urns
Simmer sultry passions;
Casseroles of deep concerns,
Sprinkled with attractions;

A succotash of salutations,
Garnished with glad, gaping grins;
Shelled and pickled stimulation's,
Smartly packed in cookie tins;

Jellied joys in crystal crocks,
Topped with adulation;
Whispers crackling on the rocks
With twists of admiration;

Pates of peppered platitudes;
A consommé of charm;
Platters heaped with attitudes
By loving thoughts kept warm;

A laughter laden leg of lamb
With curried fascination;
Tender talents glaze a ham,
Seasoned with elation;

Frappes of fleet flirtations;
Emotions coddled in a stew;
Feelings, thrills and mild sensations
Smoothly blended in a brew;

Profoundly pensive petits fours;
Blintzes bursting with respect;
Raptures daring youth explores
Served with honeyed intellect;

A pheasant, stuffed with childish whims,
Sedately under glass resides,
While a servant with commitment trims
A cake of bona fides;

Wonders breaded, seared and fried;
A hash of high hilarity;
A bristling broth of selfless pride;
A mousse of magnanimity;

Gravy smothered ecstasies;
Imagination pies;
Soufflés of fickle fantasies;
A chutney of surprise;

Gumbos crowned with accolades;
Mounds of meditation;
Delights that swirl in marinades
With minced deliberation;

A bisque of blatant blandishments;
Beauty blanched and then sautéed;
Charisma flavored condiments;
Memories spread with marmalade;

Frittadas of frivolity;
A roux of wild excursions;
Dumplings dunked in sophistry,
Dotted with diversions;

Chowders chocked with clever clues;
A philosophical fillet;
And pans of panoramic views
Enhance the succulent array.

A compote cooked with calm content;
And lush elusions steeped in wine.
To all are invitations sent,
Yet many foolishly decline.

Sustaining faith in frosting whipped
Coats crumpets, crisp and neat;
And piety in syrup dipped
Makes the rife repast complete.

Our gracious host, engaged in carving,
Replenishes each empty plate,
While people everywhere are starving.
Will discovery come too late?

Life's indeed a grand buffet,
As Auntie Mame would often shout.
So, join the feast and don't delay,
Lest ye be left without.

Dullness and depression wane,
When mystery and adventure call.
The curious from gloom refrain
And gather to the table all.

Sweet anticipation
Mingled with mystique
Provides us motivation
To strive for what we seek.

We nourish the body that we may survive,
But only when spirit is fed do we thrive.

ED PIZZELLA'S
THEATRICAL RESUME

Role/Piece/Year/Producer/Location:

John Fitzgerald in *Suds In Your Eye*, (1966); Harry Lambert in *Never Too Late*, (1967); Oscar Madison in *The Odd Couple*, (1970); and Dr. Jack Kingsley in *The Impossible Years*, (1971), all for Theatre Newington ("TN"), now Theatre Newington On Stage ("TNOS"), at the Martin Kellogg Middle School Auditorium, Newington, CT; Richard Beckley and Jabez Whittlesey in *Through The Golden Door*, (1971), the Newington Centennial Pageant at the Newington High School Auditorium, Newington, CT; Andy Hobart in *The Star Spangled Girl*, (1971), for TN at Martin Kellogg; Officer Callahan in *Three On A Bench*, (1972-1975), a one-act touring production for TN; Ambassador Magee in *Don't Drink The Water,* (1973), for TN at the Town Hall Community Theatre, Newington; George and Herbert in *You Know I Can't Hear You When The Water's Running*, (1974), for TN at the Matarese Circle Restaurant on the Berlin Turnpike in Newington and as a political benefit at the Knights of Columbus Hall on North Mountain Road in Newington; Howard Carol in *Time Out For Ginger,* (1974), for TN at the Elm Hill School Auditorium, Newington; Parker Ballentine in *Critic's Choice,* (1975), for TN at the Matarese Circle; Harry Edison in *The Prisoner Of Second Avenue,* (1976), for TN at the Indian Hill Country Club in Newington; John P. Wintergreen in *Of Thee I Sing,* (1976), and Prof. Heinrich Van Helsing in *Count Dracula*, (1976), both for TN at the Town Hall Auditorium, Newington; Prof. Heinrich Van Helsing in *Count Dracula*, (1977), for the Mark Twain Masquers at the Roberts Theater, West Hartford; Lord Caversham in *An Ideal Husband*, (1977), Jacob

351

Berman in **R.U.R.,** (1977) and the **Society Gentleman** and **McCarthy** in *Time Of Your Life*, (1977), all for the Hole In The Wall Theatre ("HITW") in New Britain; an extra in the Channel 24 CPTV series, *Mundo Real*, (1977) in Hartford; **Marco** in *A View From The Bridge,* (1977), for HITW; **Preacher Haggler** in *Dark Of The Moon*, (1978), for TN at the Indian Hill Country Club, Newington; **Emile Debecque** in *South Pacific*, (1978), **Lord Montague** in *Romeo And Juliet*, (1978), and **Padre Perez** in *Man Of LaMancha*, (1979), all for HITW; **Mel Edison** in *The Prisoner Of Second Avenue*, (1979), for the Marlborough Tavern Players at the Marlborough Tavern in Marlborough, CT; **Barney Cashman** in *The Last Of The Red Hot Lovers,* (1979), at Matty's Restaurant in Glastonbury, CT; **Franz** in *The Sound Of Music*, (1979), and **Victor Velasco** in *Barefoot In The Park*, (1979), both for the Marlborough Tavern Players; the **Cyclops** in Connecticut Public Radio's production of *The Odyssey*, (1979); **Avram** and **Lazar Wolf** in *Fiddler On The Roof*, (1979-80) for the Marlborough Tavern Players at the Marlborough Tavern in Marlborough and at the Stanley House in New Britain; **Dr. Chumley** in *Harvey*, (1981), at the New Britain Repertory Theatre, New Britain, CT; the **Defense Attorney** in *The Trial Of Jesus*, (1981), for the Lutheran Churches of New Britain; **Marco** in *A View From The Bridge*, (1982), for the Little Theatre of Manchester at East Catholic High School in Manchester, CT; **Daddy Warbucks** in *Annie*, (1983-84), for the Onstage Performers at the Embassy Room in Wolcott, CT and as a benefit at St. Mary's School in Newington; **Lester Loveless** in *Spring Follies*, (1984), for HITW; the **General** (in the *Sneeze*) and the **Father** (in *The Arrangement*) in *The Good Doctor*, (1984), for Way-Off Broadway in West Hartford, CT; **Barney Cashman** in *The Last Of The Red Hot Lovers*, (1984), for TN at the Hidden Valley Country Club in Newington; **Nathan Detroit** in *Guys & Dolls*, (1984), for the Onstage Performers at the Embassy Room in Wolcott and as a benefit at St. Mary's School in Newington; **M. Lindsay Woolsey** in *Mame*, (1984), for the Onstage performers at the Embassy Room; **Victor Velasco** in *Barefoot In The Park*, (1985), for the Onstage Performers at the Embassy Room in Wolcott and for Berlin Repertory Theatre in Berlin, CT; **Fr. Brannigan** in *Vows*, (1985), a TV movie produced by Hilltop Productions and aired on Channel 5 in Torrington and Channel 32 in Newington, Rocky Hill and Wethersfield; **Sheriff Ed Earl Dodd** in *The Best Little Whorehouse In Texas*, (1985), for the Onstage Performers at the Embassy Room, at the Popular Restaurant in Southington, CT and at the Downstairs Cabaret at Tony's Place in

Newington; **Captain Von Trapp** in *The Sound Of Music*, (1986), for the Onstage Performers at L'Auberge D'Elegance Dinner Theatre in Bristol, CT; **Nathan Detroit** in *Guys & Dolls*, (1986), for the Onstage Performers at L'Auberge D'Elegance, the Downstairs Cabaret and Cedar Run Restaurant in Cromwell, CT; **Sheriff Ed Earl Dodd** in *The Best Little Whorehouse In Texas*, (1986), and **Charlesmagne** in *Pippin*, (1987), both for the Onstage Performers at L'Auberge D'Elegance; **Lt. Fogarty** in *Chicago*, (1987), **Clifton Feddington** in *The 1940's Radio Hour*, (1987), **Mr. Welch** in *Damn Yankees*, (1987), the **Wizard** in *Once Upon A Mattress*, (1987), **Amos Babcock Bellome** in *The Fantasticks*, (1988), **Jacob** in *Joseph And The Amazing Technicolor Dreamcoat,* (1988), several characters in *Casablanca*, (1988) and **Prof. Van Helsing** in *Count Dracula*, (1988), all for Theatre One Productions at L'Auberge D'Elegance Dinner Theatre; **Victor Velasco** in *Barefoot In The Park*, (1988), for the Candlelight Players at the Beckley Dinner Theatre in Berlin; **Henry Higgins** in *My Fair Lady*, (1988), and **Mr. Mushnik** in *Little Shop Of Horrors*, (1989), both for Theatre One Productions at L'Auberge D'Elegance; **David Cook** in *Beyond A Shadow*, (1989), for S. R. Trumbull Productions at the Wallace Stevens Theater in Hartford, CT; **Sheriff Ed Earl Dodd** in *The Best Little Whorehouse In Texas*, (1989), for Theatre One Productions at the Centre Stage Dinner Theatre (JRT's) in Meriden, CT; guest appearance on *Good Old Days*, (1989), a talk show produced and hosted by Claire Lear Brown on Cox Cable Community Access Channel 32; **Horace Vandergelder** in *Hello Dolly,* (1990), for Southington Community Theatre at the Bicentennial Auditorium in Southington, CT; chorus member and servant in *Cabaret,* (1990), for Theatre One Productions at the Holiday Inn in New Britain; **Clifton Feddington** in *The 1940's Radio Hour,* (1990), for Theatre One Productions at the Ramada Dinner Theatre in New Britain; **Victor Velasco** in *Barefoot In The Park,* (1991), for the Candlelight Players at the Yankee Silversmith Dinner Theatre in Wallingford, CT; **Victor Velasco** in *Barefoot In The Park,* (1991), for Theatre One at the Ramada; **Mr. Mushnik** in *Little Shop Of Horrors,* (1991), for the New Britain Repertory Theatre in New Britain; **Andrew Carnes** in *Oklahoma,* (1991), for the Candlelight Players at the Yankee Silversmith; the **Candy Butcher** and **Second Comic** in *Sugar Babies,* (1992), **Roy Hubley** in *Plaza Suite,* (1992), **Mayor Shinn** in *The Music Man,* (1992), and **Oscar Madison** in *The Odd Couple,* (1992), all for KEM Productions at the Beckley Dinner Theatre in Berlin; an extra in a national TV commercial for Dr. Pepper,

(1992) filmed in Westport, CT; **Juan Perone** in *Evita*, (1993), **Victor Velasco** in *Barefoot In The Park*, (1993), **Max Detweiler** in *The Sound Of Music*, (1993), and **Jacob Jerome** in *Brighton Beach Memoirs*, (1993), all for KEM Productions at the Beckley Dinner Theatre; **Dave** in *There's No Excuse*, (1993), a PSA by Geomatrix Productions for the New Haven Housing Authority; **Sam Nash** and **Jesse Kiplinger** in *Plaza Suite* (1994) for the Castle Craig Players in Meriden; **Lazar Wolf** in *Fiddler On The Roof* and **Andrew Carnes** in *Oklahoma* (1994) for the Starlight Dinner Theatre in East Hartford; **Sir Edward Ramsay** in *The King And I*, (1994), **Sir Osgood Fielding** in *Sugar,* (1994), **Harry** in *70 Girls 70*, (1994), and **Buffalo Bill** in *Annie Get Your Gun*, (1995), all for KEM Productions at the Beckley Dinner Theatre; **Oscar Madison** in *The Odd Couple*, (1995), and **Jesse Kiplinger** and **Roy Hubley** in *Plaza Suite*, (1995), both for Broadway Brunch at the Bradley Sheraton, Windsor Locks, CT; **Lou Graziano** in *Breaking Legs*, (1995), for KEM at Beckley; **Victor Velasco** in *Barefoot In The Park*, (1995), for KEM at the Farmington Marriott, Farmington, CT; **Floyd Spinner** in *Love, Sex And The IRS,* (1996), the **Candy Butcher** and **Second Comic** in *Sugar Babies*, (1996) and **Roscoe Clementine** in *A Little Quickie*, (1996), all for KEM at Beckley; **Town Attorney Al Newman** in *Ralph Talk*, (1996), a TV movie by Trilogy Productions; **Victor Velasco** in *Barefoot In The Park*, (1999), **Roy Hubley** in *Plaza Suite*, (2001), and **Willie Clark** in *The Sunshine Boys*, (2002), all at the Connecticut Cabaret Theatre in Berlin.

Director's Credits:

Three On A Bench (1972-1975), a one-act touring production for Theatre Newington; **Barefoot In The Park** (1985), for the OnStage Performers at the Embassy Room in Wolcott, CT; **They're Playing Our Song** (1985), for the OnStage Performers at Tony's Place in Newington; **Barefoot In The Park** (1988), for the Candlelight Players at the Beckley Dinner Theatre and for the Berlin Repertory Theatre in Berlin; **Exit Who** (1988), for Theatre Newington; **Casablanca** (1988), for Theatre One Productions at L'Auberge d'Elegance Dinner Theatre in Bristol; **Outward Bound** (1989), for Theatre Newington; **The Best Little Whorehouse In Texas** (1990) at the Centre Stage Dinner Theatre in Meriden; **Barefoot In The Park** (1991), for the Yankee Silversmith Dinner Theatre in Wallingford and the Ramada Dinner Theatre in New Britain; **Plaza Suite** and **The Odd**

Couple (1992), for KEM Productions at the Beckley Dinner Theatre in Berlin; **Barefoot In The Park** and **Brighton Beach Memoirs** (1993), for the Beckley Dinner Theatre; **Everybody Loves Opal** (1993), for Theatre Newington; **Plaza Suite** (1994), for KEM Productions at the Waterbury Sheraton; **Barefoot In The Park** (1994), for KEM Productions at the Stamford Sheraton and for Broadway Brunch at the Bradley Sheraton in Windsor Locks; **Plaza Suite** and **The Odd Couple** (1994), for Broadway Brunch at the Bradley Sheraton; **Guys & Dolls** (1995), for the Avon Old Farms School; **Barefoot In The Park** (1995), for KEM Productions at the Farmington Marriott; **Breaking Legs** and **The Sunshine Boys** (1995), for the Beckley Dinner Theatre; co-directed **Barefoot In The Park** (1999), **Plaza Suite** (2001) and **The Sunshine Boys** (2002) at the Connecticut Cabaret in Berlin.

Producer's Credits:

Co-produced **Chicago, The 1940's Radio Hour, Damn Yankees** and **Once Upon A Mattress in** 1987 and **Joseph, Casablanca, Count Dracula, My Fair Lady** and **Little Shop Of Horrors** in 1988 at L'Auberge d'Elegance Dinner Theatre in Bristol; co-produced **The Best Little Whorehouse In Texas** and **Joseph in** 1989 at Centre Stage Dinner Theatre in Meriden; and co-produced **Cabaret, The 1940's Radio Hour, Chicago** and **Barefoot In The Park** in 1990 and 1991 at the Ramada Dinner Theatre in New Britain; co-produced **Barefoot In The Park, The Odd Couple** and **Plaza Suite** for Broadway Brunch at the Bradley Sheraton in Windsor Locks.

Miscellaneous:

Set design and construction and special effects design for many of the above; and in 1987 Mr. Pizzella was nominated as best actor in an area musical by James Ruocco, Theatre Editor of the Waterbury American.